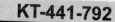

THE ESSENTIAL
Christmas
Book

Alan MacDonald and Janet Stickley

A LION BOOK
Oxford · Batavia · Sydney

Text copyright © 1992 Alan MacDonald and Janet Stickley
Colour illustrations copyright © 1992 Sarah John
This edition copyright © 1992 Lion Publishing

Published by
Lion Publishing plc
Sandy Lane West, Oxford, England
ISBN 0 7459 2032 2
Albatross Books Pty Ltd
PO Box 320, Sutherland, NSW 2232, Australia
ISBN 0 7324 0578 5

First edition 1992
All rights reserved

A catalogue record for this book is available
from the British Library

Library of Congress CIP Data applied for

Printed and bound in Singapore

Acknowledgments

'At the bottom of our street' p31 © 1992 Steve Stickley

Photographs
Howard Barlow, page 88; Barnaby's Picture Library, page 32;
Neil Beer, pages 39, 41; Adam Buchanan, pages 87, 91;
Christmas Archives, pages 9, 24 (both), 25, 28, 48 (left), 51,
54, 63; Crisis, page 30; Sonia Halliday and Laura Lushington
Photographs, pages 19, 43, 44, 55, 74/Jane Taylor, page 20;
Robert Harding Picture Library, pages 14, 34, 47, 50, 56, 68;
Lion/David Alexander, pages 8, 16/Jon Willcocks, 93; Clifford
Shirley, page 21; The Trustees of the Imperial War Museum,
page 29; Zefa (UK) Ltd, pages 23, 45, 48, 49, 73, 83, 84,
endpapers, cover.

CONTENTS

INTRODUCTION

Mention Christmas to children, and their eyes begin to sparkle. Mention Christmas to adults, and they'll probably sigh.

For many people the most joyful celebration of the year somehow gets buried under the burden of preparations—shopping, cooking, organizing visits and visitors, and trying not to worry about the expense of it all. That's why we've written *The Essential Christmas Book*—to banish the sigh and restore the sparkle to Christmas, for both adults and children. We chose the title because the book is about two things: the essentials of Christmas and the essence of Christmas.

It's about the essentials because this book covers all the main ingredients of the festive season: cards, traditions, decorations, presents, food, parties, songs and stories. It tells you how to avoid the empty imitations that the modern consumer Christmas brings, by returning to the old fun-filled tradition of doing it yourself. Christmas comes alive when you make it your own. If you've never made an Advent wreath, floating candles or rich chocolate truffles, if you've never held a One-World party or watched the children perform their own nativity play—then this book tells you how. And all in easy-to-follow instructions that don't assume unlimited time and resources.

There's a lot more besides, crammed into seven chapters—carols, quotations and poems, ideas, games and fascinating facts about where our Christmas customs come from. In fact, all the essentials for making this Christmas the best ever!

We also wanted the book to be about the essence of Christmas. At the heart of the celebration is the amazing fact that God became a child and was born into our world as the infant Jesus. Each chapter of the book introduces an event in the Christmas story, from the angels' message of peace on earth to the birth of the Prince of Peace himself.

The essentials and the essence. We hope reading and using this book will help you to rediscover the heart of Christmas—and change that sigh to a sparkle.

Alan MacDonald and Janet Stickley

GLAD TIDINGS TO YOU

CARDS TO SEND A FRIEND

The Christmas message

In the weeks leading up to Christmas perhaps the busiest person is the postman. Millions of cards are now sent every Christmas all over the world. A Christmas card is only a small piece of paper, but it is sent with love to remind friends and family that they are in our thoughts.

On the very first Christmas, God sent the angels with greetings of love to the earth. The message

they brought spoke of great joy for all people. Not only had God *sent* his message but he had also come himself—in the person of his son Jesus. John's Gospel speaks of Jesus as 'the Word made flesh'—God's message of love come down at Christmas.

'The Word became a human being and, full of grace and truth, lived among us. We saw his glory, the glory which he received as the Father's only Son.'

JOHN 1:14

"Every Christmas card tells you something about the person who sent it—that's what Grandma says. There are the funny ones and the jolly ones: top-hatted snowmen, fat chuckling Santas and oval-mouthed carol singers; the 'remember the old days' cards: stage-coaches and sledges and villagers up to their boots in snow; and the mystery ones: shepherds, wise men and grandma and me, all crowding into the hushed stable.

The first Christmas card had angels on it—or that's the way Grandma tells it. Not one or two angels, but angels everywhere like stars in the sky only brighter. And the first Christmas wishes were sung to the shepherds by a choir that sounded like all the choirs in the world bursting into song at once. And the song they sang was sung for us all: 'Glory to God and peace to all people on earth.'

'I'd like to have seen the first Christmas card,' I tell Grandma. 'Yes,' she says,'it tells you something about the person who sent it.'"

HOW CHRISTMAS CARDS BEGAN

The custom of sending Christmas cards is now so well established that it is surprising to discover that it is only about one hundred years old.

Valentine cards were popular in the mid-eighteenth century and New Year cards were exchanged in Europe a long time before Christmas cards became accepted, in the 1870s. Other early forerunners were the Christmas greetings children brought home from school, done in their best handwriting on decorated paper, to present to proud parents. Traders would also leave specially decorated visiting cards at Christmas. But it is an Englishman, Sir Henry Cole, who is credited with the idea of the first Christmas card.

Cole was the first director of the Victoria and Albert Museum in London. He was a businessman with a keen interest in art. In December 1843 he found he had little time to write individual Christmas greetings to his friends, so he decided to produce a printed card. The artist John Calcott Horsley drew a design which Cole approved, and so the first Christmas card was born. It had a picture of a family enjoying the festivities, with

Although the first commercial Christmas card was rather dull by modern standards, it marked the beginning of one of the most wide-spread Christmas customs.

two side panels showing acts of charity. One thousand of the cards were printed and sold for a shilling each.

The idea was not an overnight success. But advances in the colour printing process and the introduction of the halfpenny post for cards in the 1870s meant that Christmas cards started to gain widespread popularity in England. By 1880 the Post Office was having to broadcast its annual advice: 'Post early for Christmas', familiar to those who live in Great Britain.

At around the same time, Christmas cards were becoming popular in America through the work of Louis Prang, a German living in Massachusetts. He produced high-quality cards and helped to spread their appeal by organizing nationwide competitions for the best design.

Many of the designs still seen today originated with the earliest Christmas cards.

Snow-scenes, pictures of festive feasting and nativity scenes were all popular. Other early cards were more elaborate, coming in the shape of fans, stars or scrolls. Some even had silk finishes and pictures that could be 'animated' by pulling a tab.

Cards with the personal touch

Today, when we look back at the ingenious variety of the early Christmas cards, it is easy to feel that modern mass-produced cards lack the same originality. If you are prepared to invest a little time, rather than money, you can produce your own Christmas cards. With a simple, easily reproduced design it's possible to make home-made cards for everyone. Alternatively, you might make special cards just for close friends and family. There are a whole range of ideas in this chapter, and you don't have to be a great artist to make them!

Stand-up cards

Stand-up cards stand out from the rest for originality. Children can make these two simple cards, but younger ones will need help to cut the shapes accurately. Do bear in mind that children may need supervision when using scissors or a craft knife.

Herald angels

This card stands upright by means of a wide base and a fold down the middle.

You need:

Stiff white card
Gold pen or gold shiny paper
Scissors or a craft knife

To make:

1 First take some stiff white card and cut a piece to 15cm x 20cm. Fold the longer side in half.

2 Draw the angel shape shown here so that the fold comes at the back of the figure.

3 Cut out with scissors or a craft knife taking care to go through both halves cleanly.

4 Open out so that you have two herald angels standing back to back.

5 Decorate the angels' hair and the trumpets with a gold pen or gold shiny paper. Write your message with 'Hark the Herald Angels Sing' on the back of the card.

Pop-out Christmas tree

For many people the Christmas tree sums up the wonder of Christmas. Although the fir tree was once an object of pagan worship, its evergreen foliage is a symbol for Christians of the everlasting life promised to those who follow Christ.

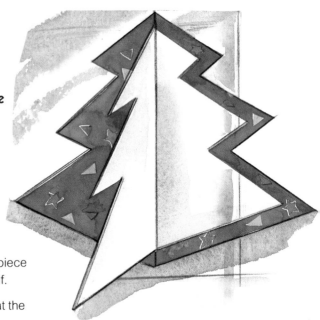

This simple stand-up Christmas tree has an unusual pop-out branches effect.

You need:

Green card
Glitter
Glue
Sticky stars and other shapes
Craft knife

To make:

1 Take a piece of green card 19cm x 25cm.

2 Draw a Christmas tree outline onto one side as shown here. Fold in half.

3 Cut along the unbroken line through

both layers and open out so that you have the tree shape.

4 Now cut along the dotted line on one side only with a craft knife. Open out.

5 You may want to decorate the tree with glitter or brightly coloured sticky stars and other shapes.

6 Write your greetings on the back of the card.

Spray and stencil

Even younger children can produce effective cards by using stencil shapes. The best results are usually achieved from the simplest shapes. Holly, stars, bells and crowns all work well.

You need:

*Thick card
Bright or dark coloured card
Thick, straight-ended brush
Poster paint or gold or silver spray paint
Paper doily
Craft knife*

To make:

1 Draw the shapes you want onto thick card, and cut out the stencil using a sharp craft knife (adults should do this part).

2 Place the stencil over a piece of coloured card.

3 Use a thick straight-ended brush and paint over the shape, or else spray paint over in gold or silver.

4 A pretty snowflake pattern can be produced by spray-painting over a small paper doily. Use gold or silver on a dark blue or black background.

5 Write your message on the back of the card.

Extra-special cards

Present card

You need:

*Brightly coloured card
Contrasting bright narrow ribbon
(with Christmas design if possible)
White paper
Scissors*

To make:

1 Cut card to 20cm x 10cm. Score with scissors and fold in half to make a 10cm square card. Cut a small slit in 'spine' at centre of fold.

2 Thread through 80cm length of ribbon and tie, parcel style, finishing with a small bow at centre front. Secure inside with a little sticky tape or strong glue.

3 Cut a 'parcel tag' from white paper. Write a message and stick in place, tucked into the bow.

4 Write personal greeting inside.

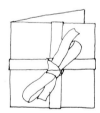

> ### Tips
>
> ★ Use glue sparingly—or it oozes out.
>
> ★ Use the right glue for the materials you are sticking.
>
> ★ Write your message with a fine pen using very small letters, or use a thick felt pen and make it really bold.

Star mobile card

You need:

Dark coloured card
Gold or silver card
Thick card
Needle and thread

To make:

1 Cut card to 20cm x 10cm. Score and fold in half to make a 10cm square card.

2 Using a craft knife, cut a 5cm diameter circle from the front flap of the card.

3 Draw and cut out a small star from thick card (see general guidelines on page 14). Using template, cut one star from gold or silver card (or card painted with gold/silver poster paint).

4 Using needle and fine thread suspend the star in the round window with a loose stitch at top point. Knot inside card to secure.

5 Write greeting on the back of the card, to keep the star mobile effect simple and uncluttered.

Bethlehem rooftops card

You need:

Dark blue or black card
Self-adhesive gold or silver stars
White cartridge paper
Fine felt pen
Glue stick
Silver pen
Craft knife

To make:

1 Cut card to 12cm x 18cm. Score and fold in half to make a 12cm x 9cm card.

2 Take a sheet of white cartridge paper 12cm x 14cm. Score and fold in half to make a shape 12cm x 7cm. Crease firmly with fingernail. Cut a 'rooftops' shape (see diagram).

3 Apply glue to back of shaded area of rooftops shape. Stick to card, lining up bottom and both vertical edges.

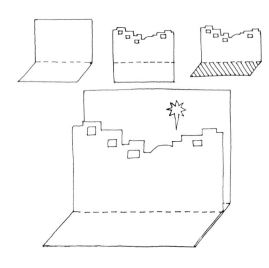

4 Add star in sky at top right hand side.

5 Write an appropriate greeting such as 'Dawn on our darkness' on 'hillside' at bottom right-hand corner in small lettering, with fine pen.

6 Add personal details on reverse of card using silver (or write message on white paper and glue on).

Stained glass window card

You need:

Stiff coloured card
Thin white paper
Felt tip pens
Cooking oil
Cotton wool
Glue stick
Matching ribbon
Craft knife

To make:

1 Make the window surround from stiff coloured card. Cut out the arch window shape with a sharp craft knife.

2 Trace the window shape onto thin white paper. Allow an extra border of 5mm all round so that it can be glued to the back of the card. Draw your own picture onto the paper. Colour in with felt tip pens.

3 To achieve a transparent effect rub cooking oil on the back of the drawing using cotton wool.

4 Glue onto the back of the card window surround. Add a ribbon so that your card can be hung in front of a window or other source of light. Finally write the Christmas greeting under the stained glass window with a fine felt tip pen.

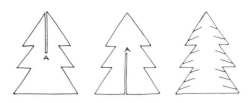

(the size you choose depends on where it will stand and how many cards you expect to receive!).

2 Using a craft knife cut a narrow slit to centre point 'A' in each as shown in the diagram.

3 Paint shapes green, silver or gold (spray paint is ideal). Allow to dry.

4 With craft knife make cuts along edges of shapes. Slot the two shapes together. Insert cards into cuts, with larger cards towards the lower branches.

Cards on display

Sometimes the first cards seem to arrive way before Christmas, especially if they're posted overseas. It's all too easy just to leave them in a pile. Displaying cards can be quite a challenge—put them on the mantelpiece or windowsill, and they're sure to fall over every time someone shuts the door!

Card tree

If you haven't got much wall space then this free-standing display could be just the thing.

You need:

Corrugated cardboard carton
Spray paint—green, silver or gold
Craft knife

To make:

1 Cut two identical large Christmas tree shapes from the sides of a corrugated cardboard carton

Ribbons and rosettes

Hang cards in vertical rows by stapling onto brightly coloured ribbon. Top off the ribbon with a big bow or rosette. Leave a tail of ribbon at the bottom cut into an inverted V-shape.

To make a star

Stars can be very difficult to draw. These instructions will help you to draw perfect stars for the activities in this book.

To make a 6-pointed star

Draw a circle using a compass. Make a mark at any point on the circle and draw a line joining it to the centre. Take a protractor and measure 6 segments of $60°$, making a mark each time on the circle. Join each mark to 2 others, as shown on the diagram on the right.

To make a 5-pointed star

Follow the directions for the 6-pointed star, but this time make 5 segments of $72°$.

Strings and things

Fasten cards with coloured paper-clips to long lengths of attractive parcel string or sparkle-effect knitting wool slung across walls from corner to corner of the room. Or attach cards to shorter crêpe paper garlands fastened across bookcases or shelves.

Climbing cards

You need:

Folding garden trellis
Green, silver or gold spray paint
Wooden clothes-pegs
Tinsel
Baubles

To make:

1 Spray trellis with green, silver or gold paint.

2 Mount on the wall or hang from the picture rail.

3 Clip cards on with painted wooden clothes-pegs. Decorate with tinsel and baubles.

Beautifully wrapped presents can make an attractive display, and often half the fun of Christmas gifts is in contemplating an exciting looking parcel and trying to guess its contents.

Whether your friends and family rip off the paper eagerly or carefully remove the sticky tape, hand-made wrapping paper can give a designer look at an everyday price.

Hand-printed paper

Potato-printing is something everyone in the family can do, even the youngest child—but a washing-up bowl of warm soapy water and a towel are essential!

You need:

1 roll of white lining paper (from DIY shops)
1 or 2 brightly coloured powder or poster paints
1 large potato
Sharp knife

To make:

1 Make a thick paint mixture (add a little wallpaper paste or washing-up liquid to make it really thick).

2 Cut the potato in half (an adult should do this) and draw a simple Christmas motif such as a star, Christmas tree or holly leaf onto the cut half with a fine felt tip pen. Cut away the potato around the design, leaving it standing out. (Pastry cutters in festive shapes provide a ready-made design when pressed into the potato.)

3 Pour the paint into an old saucer. Dab the potato into the paint and then press onto the paper at regular intervals.

4 If necessary small details can be added with a pen or paintbrush when the prints are dry.

Seasonal silhouettes

You need:

Stiff card
1 roll of white lining paper
Powder or poster paints
Small sponge
Old toothbrush
Craft knife

To make:

1 Cut out Christmas motifs from stiff card with a craft knife.

2 Lay them on the paper to form a design.

3 Gently dab on paint around the shapes using a small sponge. Continue until all the paper is covered, or using similar stencils, apply colour by flicking thin paint over them onto the paper from an old toothbrush.

Gift tags

A matching gift tag puts the finishing touches to a tastefully wrapped present. Here are several easy ways to make your own.

Matching tags

Probably the simplest way is to use left-over wrapping paper (whether bought or home-made).

You need:

Wrapping paper
Glue
Thin white card
Scissors

To make:

1 Glue the wrapping paper onto some thin white card to give it a backing.

2 Draw the shape of a bell, holly leaf, Christmas tree or other motif onto the card.

3 Cut out the shape and write your message on the plain white side.

Thumb print art

Anyone can do thumb prints, and younger children love them. All you need to do is dip a thumb in poster paint and make a print on a piece of paper. Then experiment with the print using felt pens. It can become a Christmas pudding, with a sprig of holly drawn on top; or a robin, with the addition of a tail, beak, eye and red breast. Two thumb-prints could form the body and head of a reindeer; or one the head-dress of a shepherd at the manger. The possibilities are endless. Remember, a tag should be smaller than your present!

Tags with sparkle

The most inexpensive way to make attractive-looking gift tags is to cut out pictures from old Christmas cards—small shapes such as teddy-bears, presents, crackers or snowmen are ideal.

You need:

Old Christmas cards
Ribbon or cotton
Glitter
Glue
Christmas motif stencils
Scissors

To make:

1 Cut around the shapes.

2 Add ribbon or cotton to tie.

3 Add a bit of sparkle to the picture with some glitter. Or make glitter tags:

Draw a simple Christmas symbol and spread glue within the outline. Sprinkle glitter onto the glue and shake off any excess onto a piece of paper to save for next time.

4 Don't forget your message!

Good enough to eat

What could be better than an edible gift tag? Make a gingerbread man (see Chapter 2 or Chapter 5 for special Christmas gingerbread recipes) and write the correct name on the front in icing. Prick a hole in the top and, when it is baked, add a ribbon to tie it to the present.

Present presentation

Here are some ideas to make your presents under the tree rival a shop-window display.

Christmas colours

Develop a colour theme for all your gifts. Buy packets of crêpe or tissue paper in just two or three toning colours—or shades of one colour. Wrap all your parcels in one colour and dress them with contrasting paper ribbons and bows. Or decorate with simple stick-on shapes—you could wrap all your parcels in midnight blue and stick on large stars cut from silver foil, mounted on thin card. Add a gift tag in a lighter blue or snow white for a really stunning effect.

You'd never guess...

What about those awkward shaped presents—the ones that are really difficult to disguise or turn into attractive parcels? The answer is to put them into another container—a box or a tube of cardboard will hide a give-away shape and can easily be made into an interesting package.

Shiny baubles

You need:

Tissue paper and matching crêpe paper
Cellophane
Sticky tape
Ribbon
Scissors

To make:

1 Wrap your gift in tissue paper.

2 Cut out equal sized circles of crêpe paper and cellophane and decorate the edges by trimming with scissors.

3 Lay the crêpe paper on top of the cellophane and place the gift in the centre.

4 Draw up the edges and gather in at the top.

5 Secure with sticky tape and finish with a bow.

Candle

You need:

Toilet roll or larger cardboard tube
Crêpe or tissue paper in two contrasting colours
Thin card
Orange and yellow felt tip pens
Glue or sticky tape
Scissors

To make:

1 Slip small gifts into the cardboard middle of a toilet roll. For larger gifts make a card tube.

2 Cover with crêpe or tissue paper.

3 Cut a long thin strip of contrasting colour and stick it spiral fashion from the base up to the top.

4 Cut out a card flame and colour orange and yellow. Stick in place on top of candle.

Spot on

You need:

Square box
Plain bright paper in two contrasting colours
Glue
Thin card
Scissors

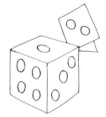

To make:

1 Cover the box very neatly with plain bright paper.

2 Make bold dots from the contrasting colour and stick them on to form the faces of a dice.

3 Make a matching gift tag by covering a folded card with the same paper and dots on the outside.

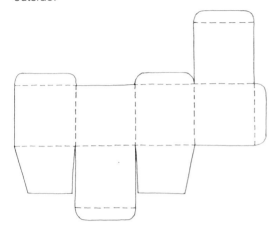

If you cannot find a suitable box—make your own, using the above guide.

1 Draw the six equal squares whatever size you need, on thin card.

2 Cut out, score the folds lightly, bend to shape and glue tabs inside. Leave one free as your lid.

Too big to wrap?

Some presents, like bicycles or household appliances, are much too big to wrap. Throw over a sheet or table-cloth, tie with a wide crêpe paper ribbon and top off with an enormous crêpe bow. Or cut out and sew on crêpe paper Christmas shapes or letters—a large 'Happy Christmas', or even the person's name. Use loose stitches, and they can easily be removed afterwards.

The final touch

Ribbons, bows and other trimmings can give that final touch which makes a parcel appear really special and luxurious. Don't skimp on ribbon—make it too wide rather than too narrow. Bows and rosettes should be too big rather than too small. Tie a present up with ribbon, securing it with a knot, then use a separate large bow or rosette to hide the knot.

To make a rosette

You need:

Self-adhesive parcel ribbon
Scissors

To make:

1 Make circles out of the ribbon, starting with a few larger circles stuck together at the middle, as shown in diagram.

2 Gradually make the circles smaller as you go round, sticking them on top of each other to form a flower-like shape.

3 Attach to parcel with sticky tape.

Other ideas

★ For a very special effect, tie sprigs of greenery or clusters of fir cones into a bow. For a child, tie in tiny packages of sweets or sticks of rock.

★ If you find ribbon too expensive—make your own from strips cut from packets of crêpe paper. Used generously, these can perk up the plainest wrapping paper. Or cut thin strips of wrapping paper and rub them firmly from top to bottom with the edge of a ruler until they curl into ribbons.

ANGELS FROM THE REALMS OF GLORY

Angels from the realms of glory
Wing your flight o'er all the earth;
Ye who sang creation's story
Now proclaim Messiah's birth:
   Come and worship,
     Worship Christ, the new-born King.

Shepherds in the fields abiding,
Watching o'er your flocks by night,
God with man is now residing,
Yonder shines the infant Light:

Sages, leave your contemplations,
Brighter visions beam afar;

Seek the great Desire of Nations:
Ye have seen his natal star:

Saints before the altar bending,
Watching long in hope and fear,
Suddenly the Lord, descending,
In his temple shall appear:

Though an infant now we view him,
He shall fill his Father's throne,
Gather all the nations to him;
Every knee shall then bow down.

JAMES MONTGOMERY (1771–1854)

19

GOOD NEWS FOR ALL
TRADITIONS OLD AND NEW

The shepherds' tale

The first Christians were not able to read about the life of Jesus. The stories about him were passed on by word of mouth until the Gospel writers wrote them down. Among these stories must have been the account of how the angels chose rough, working shepherds to be the first to hear about the miracle of God coming down to live on earth.

'And there were shepherds living out in the fields near by, keeping watch over their flocks at night. An angel of the Lord

appeared to them, and the glory of the Lord shone around them, and they were terrified.

But the angel said to them, "Do not be afraid. I bring you good news of great joy that will be for all the people. Today in the town of David a Saviour has been born to you; he is Christ the Lord. This will be a sign to you: You will find a baby wrapped in strips of cloth and lying in a manger."

When the angels had left them and gone into heaven, the shepherds said to one another, "Let's go to Bethlehem and see this thing that has happened, which the Lord has told us about."'

LUKE 2:8–12, 15

"At Christmas people spare a thought for homeless people like me. They open up church halls for us. Dole out hot soup and Christmas dinner on paper plates. I'm not complaining. It's just that the rest of the year we're easy to forget.

I like the shepherds in the Christmas story. Who gave them a second thought, out on the hills in all weathers? I bet some nights they looked down on the cosy lights in the village and wished they were snug in bed too.

But then they would have missed it all. Not just a cup of soup but the works—Christmas lights, heavenly carol singers and the sort of invitation that you couldn't buy for all the tea in China.

I bet they had stories to tell around the fire to last them the rest of their lives. Come to think of it, Jesus was kind of homeless, wasn't he?"

The Christmas celebrations in Sweden get under way on 13 December—St Lucy's day. St Lucy was a young Sicilian girl martyred for her Christian beliefs in AD 304. One legend says that during a famine she brought food to people, her head haloed in light.

On the morning of St Lucy's day, the daughter of the house dresses as St Lucy and wakes her family with hot coffee and freshly baked Scandinavian bread (*lussekatter*) or spicy gingerbread biscuits. She wears a white dress with a red sash, and a wreath on her head crowned with lighted candles (these days they aren't real!). Sometimes she is accompanied by 'Star boys' who wear pointed hats and carry wands.

St Lucy's gingerbread

Gingerbread stays fresh for some time, if stored carefully. These gingerbread hearts can be made for St Lucy's day, but will keep until Christmas. This recipe includes a delicious chocolate covering.

You need:

125g (4¹/₂ oz) ground almonds
250g (9oz) icing sugar
1tbsp honey
50g (2oz) finely chopped crystallized orange peel
2 egg whites
¹/₂ tsp ground ginger
¹/₄ tsp cinnamon
¹/₄ tsp cardamom
1tsp butter
150g (5oz) chocolate
Rice paper for base

To make:

1 Preheat oven to 180° C/350° F/Gas 4

2 Mix the almonds, icing sugar, honey and chopped orange peel. Beat egg whites till they hold stiff peaks and then fold the spices into them. Combine the two mixtures thoroughly.

3 Roll out dough onto a board generously sprinkled with sugar. Roll to 8mm (¹/₃ inch). Cut out heart shapes, dipping cutter or knife in sugar each time. Transfer them carefully to a baking tray lined with rice paper. The excess can be broken off after baking.

4 Bake 20–25 minutes. Transfer to rack to cool.

5 Melt butter and chocolate together over a pan of hot water. If the mixture seems too thick add a little hot water. Using a skewer, bore a hole in the gingerbread heart and thread with a ribbon. Dip each in chocolate and hang on a stick until dry.

Advent calendars

Children soon catch the excitement of Christmas as lights and decorations appear in town. But waiting for Christmas Day to arrive, especially once Advent has started on December 1, can seem like waiting for ever to a child. The daily ritual of marking off another day on the Advent calendar can provide a lot of pleasure—and make the days go more quickly!

Gift tree calendar

This tree not only marks off the days until Christmas, but also has a surprise treat for each day.

You need:

Felt, green and a contrasting colour
24 small gifts, for example brightly-wrapped sweets, pencil sharpeners, badges or tiny model animals
Green cotton
Needle
24 gold curtain rings
Glue
Sticky stars
Sequins
Chocolate gold coin with a king's head

To make:

1 Cut the outline of a Christmas tree out of a piece of green felt, 60cm x 40cm.

2 Thread the needle with a short length of green cotton, tape a gift to the other end and thread the cotton through the felt. Arrange the threads at regular intervals with the presents hidden behind the tree.

3 Attach the free end of each thread to a gold curtain ring. Sew another ring at the top of the gift tree so that it can be hung up.

4 Inside each ring add a number from 1 to 24. These can be cut from pieces of different coloured felt and glued on. You could also decorate the tree with stars and sequins.

5 On each day pull out a ring and cut the thread so that the present drops down to be claimed. You could use a chocolate gold coin for the 24th, with the head of a king to show that a heavenly king was born at Christmas.

Advent wreath

Another traditional way of marking the days of Advent is by making an Advent wreath. This colourful decoration, decked with ribbons and evergreens, has four candles: one to light on each Sunday of Advent. It can either be free-standing as a centrepiece to a table, or hung from the ceiling by red ribbon.

You need:

1 wire coat hanger
4 red candles
Sphagnum moss (from a florist's)
Evergreen—yew, juniper or
   cypress branches
Red satin ribbon (5cm wide)
Gardener's or florist's wire

To make:

1 A wire frame can easily be made from a coat hanger. Simply snip the hook off the hanger with wire cutters, and bend the frame into a circle.

2 Cover with sphagnum moss (available at florist's), binding it on with florist's or gardener's wire. If the wreath is to be free-standing, only cover the top of the frame.

3 Take several branches of evergreen and arrange them to cover the moss, overlapping the pieces to cover the stems. Tie them on with wire.

4 Add sprigs of holly, with berries if possible. To decorate with pine cones, wind a loop of wire around the lowest layer of the cone, and twist the two ends together around the wreath.

5 Position four red candles evenly around the circle. They can be held in place by florist's wire: gently push a length of heated wire through the candle 1.5cm above the base, and twist the two ends around the wreath.

6 If you want a hanging wreath you'll need four equal lengths of red satin ribbon 5cm wide. Tie on the ribbon at equal points between the candles and staple the ends together at the top. Make a wire loop to hang the wreath and a bow to decorate it. Also add smaller bows where the ribbons are fixed to the wreath.

Advent candle

For those who don't feel up to making something as elaborate as the Advent calendar or wreath, the Advent candle is the simplest way of marking the days up to Christmas. Like the calendar, the tradition of the candle comes from Scandinavia and Germany but is now popular the world over.

The Advent candle has twenty-four numbered sections on it. It is lit on 1 December and allowed to burn down a little more each day until it reaches the last section on 24 December.

For many families all over the world the Christmas crib, or nativity scene, is a lovely reminder of the very first Christmas. The custom is known to be at least 700 years old. One of the earliest recorded crib scenes in Europe was life-sized! On Christmas Eve, 1223, St Francis of Assisi and his followers climbed the rocky hillside above their village, where they prepared a manger. Local people came to join them, carrying burning torches and singing hymns of praise. Ox and ass were led in, and the joy and hardships of Christ's birth were re-enacted. This provided an experience for the villagers which must have been moving and inspiring, as well as reminding them of the harsh reality of what it meant for Jesus, the Son of God, to be born into a poor family.

The tradition of the crib scene is probably still strongest in the Mediterranean areas where it began. In thirteenth-century Italy, large-scale models of whole villages and towns were built, peopled with figures dressed in the ordinary clothes of the day. These *presepi* showed Jesus' birth in the context of everyday life, and helped everyone to understand its meaning for themselves.

A crib fit for a king

How many of us can remember, as children, unwrapping and setting up the figures of the holy family, shepherds, wise men and angels in a nativity scene?

Danish wooden nativity figures.

For our own children it can be a very special moment in the Christmas preparations. Sometimes a nativity scene can provide a focus for Christmas Eve. But if you want to have the scene on display longer, add the characters to it gradually throughout the Christmas season. The high spot, of course, comes on Christmas Eve when you add the baby Jesus, to take his place in the manger. Then you can move the wise men around the house or room, bringing them closer to the stable, until Epiphany (6 January) when many Christians have traditionally celebrated the wise men bringing gifts to the child Jesus.

A brightly painted crib scene from El Salvador.

Crib scenes are an important
Christmas tradition in many
countries around the world. As
shown here, styles can vary
enormously.

A simple clay crib scene from
Galicia in Spain.

Setting the scene

You need:

Strong cardboard box
Strong cardboard
Brown or black poster or emulsion paint
Blue and brown crêpe or tissue paper
Gold or silver card
2 sturdy twigs
Straw (pet's straw will do)
2 garden canes
Small twigs
Craft knife or scissors

To make:

1 Lay the box on its side with the flaps open towards you.

2 Fold the bottom flap in to strengthen the floor.

3 Fold the top flap back to form a 'sloping' roof.

4 Trim the side flaps diagonally (see diagram).

5 Cut a window in the centre of the back panel.

6 Add a semi-circular card extension at the front, to join the side flaps with an area of extra floor for your nativity figures to stand on.

7 Paint inside and out with black or brown poster or emulsion paint.

8 Stick blue crêpe or tissue paper behind the window opening, and stick on a gold or silver card star.

9 Roughly cut a wide strip of brown crêpe paper and glue onto the bottom half of the walls, right across the inside of the box, from flap to flap.

10 Stick the two sturdy twigs in position at the front corners of the stable to form supports.

11 'Thatch' the roof with straw tied in small bundles and stuck in position on roof flap. Attach a long sausage of straw to the top edge of the roof.

12 Insert two canes longer than the height of the box through the back corners, and push them into the roll of straw to support the roof at the right angle. Cover the stable floor with straw and small twigs to give a natural feel. It is ready for your figures.

Creating the characters

For a simple but effective crib scene, the cardboard figures below are ideal.

You need:

Thin card
Ping-pong or craft polystyrene balls
Felt tip pen
Glue
Fabric scraps
Brown or black wool
Tiny gifts
Matchsticks
Fur scraps
Brown or black felt
Cotton wool
Poster paints

To make:

1 Cut circles out of thin card, and make them into cones by slitting to the centre of the circle and overlapping the edges.

2 Slit both sides of each cone halfway up with a craft knife and pass through a strip of card for the arms. Cut a hand in each end of the strip.

3 Draw features onto a ping-pong ball or polystyrene craft ball with the pens. Make a hole in the ball and glue onto the pointed top of the cone. Glue on wool for hair.

4 Dress figures in simple fabric robes and cloaks, glued onto the cardboard.

5 Stick gifts for the wise men and matchstick crooks for the shepherds to their hands with strong glue.

6 Cut animal shapes from double thicknesses of card, with a fold along the top edge so that they will stand. Stick on fur, felt or cotton wool.

Clay figures

For a set of figures you can keep, use self-hardening modelling clay or homemade salt dough (see page 28 for recipe), which is easy enough for younger children to handle.

To make:

1 Make conical bodies, about 50mm (2in) high and 50mm (2ins) across the base, from fat sausages of dough.

2 Roll a 25mm (1in) ball for the head and secure with a wooden cocktail stick, sticking in place with a little egg white. (Make the figures a little taller and thinner than you want them to end up, to allow for settling.)

3 Roll out flat sheets of dough and cut cloaks to drape over wise men, and head-dresses for other characters.

4 Make turbans and headbands from lengths of thin dough 'piping', and gifts from spheres, cubes and pyramids of dough. Stick details in place with egg white.

5 Make animal shapes, strengthening where necessary with cocktail sticks. Finish off sheep with dough 'wool' pushed through a metal sieve.

6 Leave the figures to harden overnight, then put in an extremely cool oven (200˚F/100˚C/Gas Mark 1) for three to four hours. If the oven is too hot, the bases may swell. If so, level them off with a craft knife.

7 Paint with poster colours using a very fine brush for the details. Leave the flesh as natural dough colour.

Salt dough

Use instead of modelling clay to make figures for a crib scene.

You need:

2 cups plain flour
2 cups salt
2 tbs wallpaper paste (make sure it doesn't contain fungicide)
1 cup water

To make:

1 Mix ingredients together and knead to form a smooth dough.

2 Shape into characters for the crib scene.

3 Leave overnight to harden before baking in a very low oven (200° F/100° C/Gas Mark 1) for 3–4 hours until dried out.

Peruvian crib

Make the relevance of Christmas really come alive for your family and friends, by including them in your crib scene. You could also add pets, neighbours, local shopkeepers, figures representing local industries and crafts, favourite animals and, of course, yourself. Make the figures out of clay or salt dough.

This crib scene from Peru includes figures from everyday life as well as the traditional characters of the Christmas story.

PEACE ON EARTH, GOODWILL TO ALL

Peace on earth

The time was Christmas Day morning, 1914; the scene was 'no man's land', between the German and British front-line trenches in the First World War. Soldiers, German and English, who yesterday had been killing each other, were standing together, shaking hands, taking photographs and exchanging cigarettes.

German and British officers during the unofficial truce on Christmas Day, 1914.

It was a welcome, unexpected, respite from violence and hatred. Although it was only a temporary truce, they were pausing to celebrate the coming of Jesus the peacemaker.

Sometimes family occasions are a bit like temporary truces in a war which should have long since come to an end! Could a simple card sent to an estranged friend, or half an hour given to quiet conversation with an elderly or difficult relative help further the process of healing old hurts or misunderstandings?

Goodwill to all

While Christmas for many is a time of plenty and friendship, it can highlight the poverty or loneliness of some people's lives. December 26 celebrates the Feast of St Stephen, or Boxing Day as it is known in Britain. It was on this day, we are told in the song, that Good King Wenceslas looked out:

> *Good King Wenceslas looked out*
> *On the Feast of Stephen,*
> *When the snow lay round about*
> *Deep and crisp and even.*
> *Brightly shone the moon that night,*
> *Though the frost was cruel;*
> *When a poor man came in sight*
> *Gathering winter fuel.*

King Wenceslas took the man food, drink and firewood, to cheer and warm him with the spirit of Christmas.

Christmas is a time when people have traditionally been reminded to think of others and give generously to the poor. In Britain, Boxing Day originally got its name from the custom of distributing the money put in alms boxes for the poor people in a town or parish. The day after Christmas, the boxes were broken open and the money distributed by the priests. This custom, which dates back to Roman times, was stopped during the Protestant Reformation in the sixteenth century. 'Christmas Boxes' then became gifts of money, or tips, given to servants, tradespeople and those who had provided services throughout the year.

Many charitable organizations make a special effort at Christmas to make sure the homeless and needy are not left out of the festivities.

A time to share

Today we can express our care for others at Christmas time in practical ways. Many people are lonely, housebound or unable to afford the luxuries of food and drink that we may take for granted at Christmas. Perhaps there is room at our table for someone who would appreciate being included in our celebrations.

We can give money or time to Third World aid organizations or those who work with homeless people.

★ We can give toys and other gifts to deprived families through local organizations or Social Services.

★ We can take a Christmas dinner to a housebound neighbour.

★ We can invite someone we know who will be alone on Christmas Day to share the day with us.

★ We can help at parties and Christmas meals in hospitals or old people's homes.

★ We can provide transport to Christmas events for elderly or housebound people.

★ We can buy or sell cards and other goods from charity gift catalogues.

AT THE BOTTOM OF OUR STREET

At the bottom of our street Arthur works,
I've seen him lots of times with black-caked hands
Under the bonnets of cars and vans
He laughs and swears and sometimes spits.
I've seen him pulling cars to bits
Then weld them back together again,
Smoke a fag, drink some tea,
And once he even winked at me,
at the bottom of our street.

At the bottom of our street there's a sign:
'Arthur's Garage, please drive in'
Whenever I've passed it there's such a din
Spanners dropping, hammering, radio blaring
  classic rock hits
And there's Arthur, still pulling cars to bits.
They come in crumpled, they go out sleek.
Every day of every week, Arthur's there,
Earning a living as best he can
at the bottom of our street.

At the bottom of our street one night
A baby cried, so me and me mates we went to
  check.
Danny calls out 'Flippin' eck!
Someone's left Arthur's doors undone!'
And in he popped full of fun.
We all followed, sheepish like,
Till Titch tripped over a motorbike.
'Sh!' we hiss as we try to peep at the baby born
at the bottom of our street.

At the bottom of our street we saw
A mum and child in quiet siesta
Getting warm in the back of a Ford Fiesta.
The dad said, 'As maternity goes this lacks
  quite a bit,
But eternity knows that a flame has been lit.'
He talked of a king so we minded our manners.
A king that was born surrounded by spanners?
It's funny what happens when you least expect it
at the bottom of our street.

At the bottom of our street there came
Some car mechanics to offer a toast,
They'd been in at their local 'The Heavenly Host'.
When they heard of the birth they were filled
  with euphoria.
(They said they were told by someone called
  Gloria.)
After raising a glass they started to pray,
Danny said 'Time for a quick getaway!'
So we sneaked out and left that peculiar scene
at the bottom of our street.

At the bottom of our street we stared
As three limousines came gliding by.
Out hopped three fellas all starry-eyed.
With security guards they popped inside to the
  baby king.
On greasy floor kneeling they gave their gifts
  then started to sing!
With camel-hair coats and jewellery galore
They hopped in the limos and slammed the doors
Speeding away as quick as they came
from the bottom of our street.

At the bottom of our street Arthur works,
I've seen him lots of times with black-caked hands
Under the bonnets of cars and vans
He laughs and swears and sometimes spits.
I've seen him pulling cars to bits
Then weld them back together again.
'Oi! Listen! God's come down to men!'
Called Arthur supping at his tea.
Was he joking as he winked at me,
at the bottom of our street?

STEVE STICKLEY

THE BRIGHTEST STAR

DECORATIONS THAT SPARKLE

Star in the heavens

The star that appeared in the East to herald the birth of Christ and lead the wise men to the stable is an enduring symbol of Christmas. Among all the other decorations, the Christmas star has pride of place in many households.

The Christmas story is about light dawning in a dark world, the coming of a Saviour. That star was the first bright messenger to bring the news.

'The people walking in darkness have seen a great light; on those living in the land of the shadow of death a light has dawned.

'For to us a child is born, to us a son is given, and the government will be on his shoulders. And he will be called Wonderful Counsellor, Mighty God, Everlasting Father, Prince of Peace.'

ISAIAH 9:2, 6

"Let me tell you. It's not so hot being a movie star sometimes. I mean, people can't leave you alone. In restaurants, at the theatre, even at the dentist's—there's always someone staring at you. Pointing and nudging their friends, 'Hey look it's ... you know ... isn't it? No kidding. It's her.'

Thing is—if I died tomorrow, which of them's going to remember me? Next day they'll have found someone else to point at.

At nights I like to go out on my balcony and just look at the sky full of stars that have been around for centuries. If we're talking about fame there's only one contender—the Star of Bethlehem. Now that's the kind of star I'd like to have been. People'd say, 'Hey look at her. She's the one who showed the way to where Jesus was born.'

Nobody forgets that star."

Star cluster

These easy-to-make stars have a three-dimensional effect and can be hung in shiny clusters from the ceiling or as Christmas tree decorations.

You need:

Star template (see page 14)
Shiny coloured foil
Scissors
Ruler
Darning needle
Thin cord

To make:

1 Use the 6-pointed star shape on page 14 to cut out up to 5 star shapes for each cluster from shiny coloured foil.

2 Use scissors and a ruler to score the folds in each star (see diagram). Fold the star in half along opposite points and then opposite angles. Every angle and point should have a fold when you have finished.

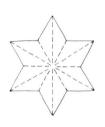

3 Now bend the star out into its three-dimensional shape. Make a hole through the middle of each star with a darning needle. Thread some cord through the centre of the stars, keeping them apart by making knots in the cord. Allow enough cord to hang the star cluster, and make a loop in the top.

Star turn

A giant glittering star made from gift wrap, to hang in a hallway or on a door.

You need:

2 pieces of shiny wrapping paper in contrasting colours, for example silver/gold or red/green
Matching ribbon
Strong glue
Thin card
Scissors
Small stapler

To make:

1 Cut out 6 triangles from each piece of wrapping paper. Make the long side of each triangle 30cm and the short sides 20cm.

2. Roll up each of your 12 triangles into cone shapes, and glue with a strong glue (see diagram).

3 Cut a small circle of 5cm diameter out of card. Arrange the cones on top of your circle to give a star shape, with the open ends pointing out. Stick or staple the thin ends of the cones to the card circle in the middle.

4 Add a finishing touch with lengths of ribbon in the middle in matching colours. Allow about 30cm of ribbon each and curl the ribbon by drawing it several times along the flat blade of a pair of scissors.

LIGHT UP THE TREE!

'I have been looking on this evening, at a merry company of children assembled round that pretty German toy, a Christmas tree . . . It was brilliantly lighted by a multitude of little tapers; and everywhere sparkled and glittered with bright objects.'

CHARLES DICKENS, *HOUSEHOLD WORDS*, 1850

Legend has it that St Boniface, a Christian missionary to northern Germany, introduced the Christmas tree in the first place. The story is told that St Boniface came upon a group of pagans about to sacrifice a young boy to a great oak tree they were worshipping. Enraged, St Boniface chopped down the oak, and found a small spruce growing among its roots. He presented it to the child, saying 'Let this little evergreen tree be your symbol of everlasting life.' From that time the spruce became the focus of Christmas celebrations in north Germany.

By Charles Dickens' day, the Christmas

tree had become a firm favourite in Britain. Prince Albert, Queen Victoria's husband, brought the custom from his homeland for the delight of the royal children at Windsor Castle. Today the Christmas tree is a world-wide symbol of Christmas in every house and public place.

Ten tips for a perfect tree

★ If you wish to keep a tree for more than one year, choose one with healthy roots. Plant it in a tub lined with crocks or stones for drainage and fill with a mixture of peat and soil.

★ When buying a tree without roots, look for a symmetrical shape, good colour and healthy branches. Bounce it on the ground. If needles fall off everywhere, the tree is nearly dead.

★ Keep the tree outdoors in water until it is needed.

★ When you install it, choose a position away from any fires and leave a clear passage through the room.

★ Make sure the tree is secure so that it won't topple under the weight of decorations. Use bricks at the base of the tub, and cover with wet sand.

★ Spray with an anti-desiccant to delay drying out and loss of needles. A wise safety precaution is to use a fire-retardant spray.

★ Remove any broken twigs or branches with secateurs.

★ Decorate the tub before attending to the tree itself, otherwise you may knock off fragile decorations.

★ Check that lights work before displaying them on the tree. Work from top to bottom when adding them to the tree.

★ Decorate the tree from top to bottom and all the way round, to give a depth of colour.

DRESSING THE TREE

In some families, dressing the tree is a time-honoured ritual. Memories are unwrapped and lifted out with each decoration. In other families, it is a challenge of style and innovation. Here are some suggestions for each of these approaches, plus an alternative to a tree for those who like to be really different!

A memory tree

★ A special star or angel at the top.

★ Lights to twinkle in the dark.

★ Lots of tinsel garlands to reflect the lights.

★ Home-made decorations, added to (or replaced) each year.

★ Let young children choose a special decoration to be 'theirs'—when they leave home they will take it with them to go on their own tree.

★ Bring back little mementoes of summer holidays which can be tied with ribbon onto your tree—if you holiday abroad, you can create an international flavour.

A tree with style

★ Dress a tree using just one or two colours. Favourites are red, green, white, silver and gold.

★ Tie large ribbon bows onto branch ends. Leave long ends hanging down to give a luxurious feel.

★ Use lengths of lace to tie bows.

★ Add plain, shiny baubles and lengths of shiny beads.

★ Artificial silk (or even real) flowers can be wired and fastened onto the branches.

★ Heap small empty boxes wrapped in your choice of coloured paper around the base of the tree.

Light of the world

For an interesting alternative to a tree, a household without young children might enjoy this display of light.

Take an old pair of step-ladders, and paint them all over in a Christmassy colour. Collect together (or make) different shapes and sizes of candle, and arrange them on the steps. This looks particularly effective in the corner of a large room.

Tree-mendous decorations

Here are ideas for making tree decorations from paper, clay, fabrics or natural materials. Simply decide what sort of tree you want.

Peace on earth

This simple but effective shape can be cut out from white card and hung from the tree with silver or gold thread. You could use this shape to make a mobile as well.

Cut it out

Using self-hardening clay or salt dough (see page 28) you can make all sorts of models for your tree. The simplest way of doing this is to roll it out like pastry and cut out shapes with festive pastry cutters. Paint with poster paints and varnish before hanging with coloured ribbon.

Trees of the greenwood

★ Paint pine cones with brightly coloured poster paint. Dab tips with glue and dip into glitter.

★ Glue acorns firmly into their cups and paint with gold or silver paint.

★ Remove beech nuts from their cases, wrap in silver foil and glue back into place.

★ Spray or paint individual holly leaves with gold or silver paint. Using a large needle, thread 4 or 5 of them onto a piece of narrow ribbon. Bunch them together, tying the ribbon off into a decorative bow.

Shepherd's star

For those who can do basic crochet stitches here is a star shape to make from white or silver thread

To make

1 2 ch

2 Round 1: 5 dc in 2nd ch from hook.

3 Round 2: 3 dc in each dc.

4 Round 3: (1 dc in next st, 6 ch, ss in 2nd ch from hook, 1 dc in next ch, 1 htr in next ch, 1 tr in next ch, 1 dtr in next ch, 1 dtr in base of starting dc, miss 2 dc) 5 times, ss in first dc to join.

5 Fasten off.

The star of the show

Make a sparkling star to top your tree.

You need:

Wooden cocktail sticks
Plasticine or modelling clay
Thin card
Scissors
Gold or silver spray paint, or large star-shaped sequin
Glue or strong sticky tape
Green garden twine or wool

To make:

1 Stick cocktail sticks into a central piece of plasticine (or modelling clay) to achieve an effect like the spokes of a wheel.

2 Cut out a card star to cover the central disc. Stick it on. Spray the whole decoration with gold or silver paint, or use a large star-shaped sequin in the centre as a finishing touch.

3 Attach green garden twine (or wool) to the back of the star with glue or strong sticky tape, and tie onto the top branch of your tree.

ENDURING EVERGREENS

The holly and the ivy,
When they are both full grown,
Of all the trees that are in the wood,
The holly bears the crown.

The rising of the sun,
And the running of the deer,
The playing of the merry organ,
Sweet singing in the choir.

The holly bears a berry,
As red as any blood,
And Mary bore sweet Jesus Christ
To do poor sinners good.

TRADITIONAL ENGLISH CAROL

From the earliest times, evergreens have been honoured and prized as decorations. Holly, ivy, mistletoe, yew, bay, laurel and rosemary—with their ability to endure through the winter when all other trees are dying—collected a whole host of superstitions around them. As early as the Roman era, evergreens were given as good luck tokens during the celebration of Saturnalia, the winter festival. Mistletoe was seen as a symbol of everlasting love, and ivy was brought into the house to ward off evil spirits.

The early Christians adopted some evergreens as symbols of their faith. The jagged leaves of the holly and its red berries reminded them of the crown of thorns Christ wore on the cross, and the blood he shed to save humanity. In Scandinavia, holly is known as the Christ-thorn.

The tradition of hanging wreaths of evergreen, pine cones and nuts on the front door originated in Scandinavia as a symbol of peace and renewal. It later became very popular in the United States.

As Christmas celebrations spread to countries across the world, other plants, including ferns, mosses and palms, were adopted into the festivities. One of the most popular Christmas plants today is the poinsettia with its bright red leaves. The Mexicans call it the Flower of the Holy Night, because its shape resembles the Star of Bethlehem.

Evergreen garland

In America, Canada and Scandinavia, natural evergreen garlands not only deck the halls but decorate the outside of houses. Many people think that such intricate-looking garlands must be difficult to make but, with a little practice, anyone can weave their own garland.

You need:

A variety of evergreen branches
Rope—about the thickness of skipping rope
Secateurs
Green gardening string and wire
Rubber gloves to protect your hands

To make:

1 Measure with the rope the size you want the garland to be, in the place where you want it to hang. Allow extra rope for a loop at each end from which to hang the garland. Tie strong loops before you begin weaving.

2 Cut the evergreen to lengths of about 20cm with secateurs.

3 Bind the evergreen to the rope in bunches of about 6 sprigs, using the green string. Keep the leaves packed together and all lying in one direction. Don't skimp on the amount of evergreen, or the garland will look mean and sparse.

4 When the garland is finished, you can wire on cones, ribbons or other decorations. Thread the wire around the base of a cone and twist the ends together before attaching to the garland.

5 Nail or tie garland in position using the loop. Spray occasionally with a fine plant spray, to prevent drying.

Wreathed in smiles

Christmas is a time for sharing, for opening our homes and inviting others to celebrate with us. So don't hang a 'no room' sign on your door. Instead, make your front door a sign of welcome to others by hanging up one of these cheerful wreaths. A brass hook screwed into your door may be the best way to secure the wreath.

Christmas night wreath

You need:

Thin card
Glue
20cm blue fabric
20cm green fabric both 90cm wide
40cm medium-weight wadding
Scissors
Needle
Thread
Felt pieces, different colours
Gold or silver fabric
Metric graph paper
Tracing paper

To make:

1 Using the diagram on the right, draw a pattern to correct size (1sq = 4cm). Place fold of tracing paper on fold of pattern, trace and cut out round outline. Open out to form ring.

2 Following the solid line on the pattern, cut one ring of wadding and one of card. Following the dotted line on the pattern, cut half a ring each of the blue and green fabrics. Stitch blue and green fabrics together to form a circle.

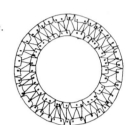

3 Lay wadding, then fabric, on top of the card ring. Cut notches in the edges of the fabric as shown, then draw edges of fabric together across the back of the card, using needle and thread.

4 Cut out star shape from card, stick onto gold or silver fabric and trim leaving small seam allowance. Cut notches in the edges as above, and stick around the back of the card.

5 Cut smaller stars from gold or silver fabric and other shapes from felt (use fluffed-out wadding for sheep's bodies), and stick all shapes in position on ring.

DECK THE HALLS!

Decorations to make

Everyone can make paper decorations. They can be as simple as paper chains, or as intricate as a hanging mobile. In Denmark there is a special 'cut and stick' day when family and friends all sit round the table adding their own contributions to the Christmas decorations. Of course, it would be easier to go out and buy shop decorations, but the Danes would say that would be missing out on half the fun of Christmas.

Chain reaction

Children often make simple link chains out of ready-cut coloured paper you can buy in the shops. The effect, however, is often rather disappointing and dreary. It is much better to use bright coloured foil paper, which is stronger and catches the light attractively.

You need:

Coloured foil paper
Double-sided sticky tape
Scissors

To make:

1 Cut lots of strips in different colours about 18cm x 3cm.

2 Stick the ends of a strip together with double-sided tape to make the first link in your chain.

3 Thread a different coloured strip through your first link, and stick the ends together in the same way.

4 Continue until the chain is the length you want, alternating colours as you go.

Hanging hearts

Paper hearts are a traditional Danish decoration. This version can be hung on its own, or as part of a mobile.

You need:

Stiff red card
Craft knife
Glue
Strong red thread

To make:

1 Cut out a heart shape from stiff red card about 10cm x 10cm.

2 Draw the outline again twice inside the shape, with 1.5cm between each outline.

3 Cut round each of the heart shapes with a craft knife. Then remove the middle section, leaving the outer and inner heart shapes.

4 Glue strong fine red thread vertically down the centre of the decoration, leaving enough spare at the top to hang it by. When the glue is dry, the central heart will move gently in its frame.

Glittering star mobile

A simple but effective mobile can be made from cardboard stars covered with glitter.

You need:

Coloured foil paper
Glue
Glitter
Thin wooden rod about 30cm long
Strong thread
Darning needle
Ribbon

To make:

1 Cut out a star shape from coloured foil. (You can use the template on page 14.) Before folding the stars into their three-dimensional shapes, coat both sides with glue and glitter. Make 10 stars in this way.

2 Tie strong thread around one end of the rod, and thread it through a point of one star, using a darning needle. Repeat until you have 2 stars hanging at either end of the mobile, and 2 sets of 3 in the middle.

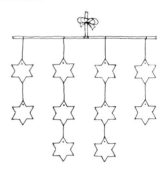

3 Suspend the mobile by a ribbon bow or thread in the middle.

Hanging lanterns

These miniature lanterns are easy enough for a child to make, and can be hung from garlands or on the Christmas tree.

You need:
Coloured foil paper
Scissors
Glue

To make:

1 Take a piece of coloured foil paper 11cm x 7cm. Cut vertical slits (shown as solid lines in the diagram). Fold along the dotted lines and then open out.

2 Glue the two ends together so that you have a circular lantern with the slits running vertically.

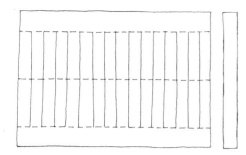

When it is dry, press gently on the top to make the sides push outwards.

3 Finally, add a handle with a strip 13cm x 1cm. Glue it on at each end inside the top of the lantern.

Starry night

Whatever special food you decide to eat on Christmas Day, you can make the meal feel really festive by the way you decorate the table. Here are some ideas for inexpensive table decorations.

Pride of place

You need:
Plain coloured fabric or felt in 2 contrasting colours
Pinking shears
Yellow or white felt
Sequins
Needle
Matching thread
Glue

To make:

1 Cut a piece of plain coloured fabric (45cm x 33cm) to form a table mat. Make a 1cm hem on all edges—or cut the piece from felt using pinking shears.

2 Cut a 10cm x 10cm piece from a contrasting colour, and a star motif from yellow or white felt.

3 Stitch a few shiny sequins onto the star, before sticking or sewing it to the smaller piece.

4 Hem smaller piece with narrow hem (unless using felt) and stitch around 3 sides onto place mat, to form a pocket for the napkin.

Stand-up stars

Use these as decorations, or write on them in waterproof ink to make place cards for a Christmas dinner party.

Cut out 2 identical stars (see page 14). Spray them gold on both sides and cut one slit in each as shown. Turn at right-angles to each other and slot together.

Star lights

Make candle holders by spraying tiny glass jars (used for meat and fish paste) gold, and decorating with coloured gummed paper stars. Hold the candles in position using a small lump of children's modelling clay or adhesive putty.

Arrange them on a lacy paper doily sprayed gold, to form an attractive centrepiece for your table.

Starry napkin rings

Stick a card star onto a cardboard ring cut from a toilet roll middle, and spray gold or silver.

THE FIRST NOWELL

The first nowell the angel did say
Was to certain poor shepherds in fields as
    they lay;
In fields where they lay a-keeping their
    sheep,
On a cold winter's night that was so deep.
    Nowell, nowell, nowell, nowell!
    Born is the King of Israel.

They looked up and saw a star
Shining in the east, beyond them far;
And to the earth it gave great light,
And so it continued both day and night.

And by the light of that same star
Three wise men came from country far;
To seek for a king was their intent,
And to follow the star wherever it went.

Then entered in those wise men three
Full reverently upon their knee,
And offered there in his presence
Their gold and myrrh and frankincense.

Then let us all with one accord
Sing praises to our heavenly Lord,
Who hath made heaven and earth of nought,
And with his blood mankind hath bought.

TRADITIONAL ENGLISH

43

BEARING GIFTS

PRESENTS FOR ALL

The first Christmas gifts

'Jesus was born in the town of Bethlehem in Judea, during the time when Herod was king. Soon afterwards, some men who studied the stars came from the east to Jerusalem and asked, "Where is the baby born to be the king of the Jews? We saw his star in the east and we have come to worship him."'

MATTHEW 2:1–2

"I blame the wise men: Balthazar, Melchior and the other one whose name I can never remember. If it wasn't for them we wouldn't have to go through all this, would we? Christmas shopping—the most painful torture ever devised.

Every year I promise myself it'll be different. I'll be organized. Make a list. Shop before the rush. Every year I find myself wedged in a crowd of bad-tempered shoppers on Christmas Eve, none of us with the least idea of what we're looking for.

I wonder what Balthazar, Melchior and thingummy would make of it all today? The special 'Xmas' offers, the credit cards, the fighting for parking space, the 'present for so and so because they always get me one although really you know I can't stand them'.

You can imagine the wise men on their camels outside the superstore, pointing to a star in the sky and saying, 'Look! It's this way. The gift from Heaven. Follow us!'

And everyone would bustle past them with their bags, grumbling, 'People will go to any lengths at Christmas to sell you something new.'"

We know very little about the wise men who came from the east to worship Jesus in Bethlehem. They are often called the three kings, but the Bible calls them Magi, wise men who studied the stars, science, philosophy and mathematics. Tradition holds that there were three of them, because of the three gifts that they brought: gold, frankincense and myrrh. Today they may seem strange presents for a child, but each of the gifts had its own significance. Gold is a gift for royalty; this was a sign that Jesus is the King of all kings. Frankincense is used in worship, and reminds us that Jesus is Emmanuel—God come down to us. Myrrh—the strangest present of all—is a spice used in burial. Even at his birth there is a hint of Jesus' coming death as the Saviour of the world.

Gold I bring . . .

Perhaps gold is a little outside your price range, but you can give very attractive home-made jewellery, with a friend's particular style or favourite colours in mind. Earrings and brooches can be made from easy-to-use modelling clay, available from most craft shops in lots of bright colours.

Personalized badges or brooches in animal shapes, or something which matches a friend's interests or hobby—tennis racket and ball, crossed knitting needles, and so on—make good presents. Glue on a brooch pin bought at your local craft shop.

Frankincense to offer

Instead of relying on man-made scents out of an aerosol, why not take advantage of some of the fragrances of nature? Bowls of spring bulbs offer the promise of sweetly-scented flowers to come. Or make a traditional pomander.

You need:
1 orange
A large packet of whole cloves
Ground cinnamon
Orrisroot powder (found in herbalists and some drug-stores)
About 70cm each of white tape and decorative ribbon
Pins, tinsel and small decorations such as tiny bells and flowers

To make:

1 Wrap white tape around orange twice to mark off quarters with a cross shape at the top and bottom of the fruit. Pin in place.

2 Using a thick blunt needle or spike, make holes all over the quarters of orange left showing. Stick in cloves.

3 Roll orange in a mixture of orrisroot powder and cinnamon. Wrap in grease-proof paper and leave in a warm place for a few weeks.

4 Remove tape and pin ribbon in its place with a loop at one end to hang it by. Decorate with tinsel and attach ornaments at the base of the loop.

Myrrh is mine

Spices and herbs are more commonly used for cooking today. With a little forethought, inexpensive gifts can be literally home-grown. Pots of herbs, grown over the summer, add useful and decorative colours to a cook's kitchen window sill.

LEADING LIGHTS

Candles bring a special warmth to any occasion, and nearly every home lights at least one candle at Christmas.

Candles, torches and Yule logs were all once part of pagan mid-winter festivals. They were lit in the darkest part of the year, in the hope that they would bring back the light and life of springtime.

Christians see the same light as representing Jesus—the Light of the world, sent by God to conquer the darkness of evil. Zechariah, a wise old man who describes the birth of Jesus in Luke's Gospel, says 'The rising sun will come to us from heaven to shine on those living in darkness.'

Christmas tree lights, stars, candles and lanterns brighten our darkness, reminding us of the Light of the world born at Christmas.

Candles can make beautiful presents for children or adults. They can be amusing decorations in festive shapes, and sophisticated gifts, given in dessert or wine glasses. Floating candles add the final touch to the atmosphere of a festive table set for guests.

Unusual candles can be expensive to buy, and many people are discovering that making their own candles is easy—and a lot more fun. This is something children will enjoy, but they need adult supervision throughout.

Make a candle

All the ingredients for candle-making can be bought from art and craft shops.

You need:

Candle wax—bought in powder or granules, or recycled from the stumps of old candles
Stearin to harden the wax
Several lengths of medium wick—string will do
as long as it is not a man-made fibre
Empty plastic pot for a mould
An old saucepan

To make:

1 Melt 9 parts of wax to 1 part stearin in an old pan over hot water.

2 Cut a length of wick, tie one end of it to a pencil and dip the wick briefly into the melted wax to coat it.

3 Lay the pencil across the mould so the wick hangs down to the centre. Fix it in place with a blob of melted wax or some plasticine.

4 Pour melted wax gently into the centre of the mould. If a dip appears around the wick, add a little more melted wax. Leave to cool. Trim the wick.

Marbled candles

A marbled effect can be achieved with a plain candle and wax crayons, though special paints for marbling are also available at craft shops.

You need:

Plain candle
Wax crayons
Saucepan of water

To make:

1 Boil some water in a saucepan.

2 Put small pieces of crayon into the water, where it will melt and form runny blobs. Let it cool slightly, and then swirl the candle around in the hot water, holding it by the wick.

3 Remove it, and dip the other end of the candle into the water. It will set at once in a marbled effect. You can experiment with one or more colours.

Snowball candles

Candles in festive shapes such as snowballs are fun as decorations, and easy to make.

You need:

One-third plain white candle (or stump of an old one)
White wax
Saucepan of water
Small basin

1 Fix candle onto a dish with a drop of melted wax.

2 Melt some white wax and a little stearin over hot water. Pour the melted wax into a small basin, and whip it with a fork.

3 Before the wax cools, press it around the candle stump into a snowball shape.

Floating candles

Small and light, floating candles are made using little bun tins or fancy pastry cutters. The wick does not need to go right through, so hold it in the centre of the soft wax during setting, until it is secure. To stop the wax leaking out of pastry cutter moulds, press them into self-hardening modelling clay, wiped with oil. Leave candles for at least twenty-four hours to harden completely.

Unusual candles can be expensive to buy. Many people are discovering that making their own is easy—and a lot more fun!

GIFT GIVING WORLD·WIDE

What we know of the first Christmas comes exclusively from the Bible, but over the centuries, many traditions have grown up which have become an essential part of the celebrations. Some customs seem to have little to do with celebrating the birth of Jesus, but often their roots lie deep in early Christian tradition with figures such as St Nicholas, the saintly Archbishop of Myra.

Every country has its own Christmas gift-giving customs, which are passed down from generation to generation until no one can quite remember how they first started.

★ In Holland, the Christmas season begins on 6 December with the arrival of St Nicholas by steamer at the port of Amsterdam. St Nicholas is dressed in a bishop's robe and mitre and is always accompanied by Black Peter who represents the devil. It is Black Peter's job to punish naughty children, and to do the dirty work of delivering presents down the chimney. Presents are actually exchanged on St Nicholas Eve (5 December), and the Dutch like to include an element of surprise. Sometimes a little gift is wrapped in a huge box, or the parcel is hidden in an unexpected place.

★ In Germany, the legend of St Nicholas has taken a different turn. He is not the present-giver, but merely the messenger who takes children's requests up to heaven. It is the *Christkind* or Christ-child who delivers the presents, dressed in white robes and a golden crown. Letters for the *Christkind* are left on window sills, and often decorated with sugar to make them sparkle.

★ Homes in Mexico are decorated in time for the beginning of *Posadas*, the season when people remember Mary and Joseph's search for somewhere to stay. Decorations may include Spanish moss, evergreens and coloured lanterns. In one corner of the room, a crib will be left for the Christ-child. Later, children look forward to the *Piñata* game. The *Piñata* is an earthenware jar, decorated with paper and streamers to look like a brightly-coloured bird or animal. Children are blindfolded, and try, one by one, to break the jar with a stick. Sometimes the *Piñata* is only filled with

St Nicholas greets excited children in Holland. (You can also see Black Peter in the crowd.)

The *Christkind* is the gift-bringer in Germany.

water or confetti, but the child lucky enough to break the right jar gets a windfall of sweets, toys and nuts. A scramble follows, with everyone trying to get as much as possible! (There are instructions for making your own *Piñata* on page 51.)

★ In Spain, presents are given at the feast of the Epiphany or Twelfth Night (6 January). *Los Reyos Magos*—the three kings—will often parade through the town giving out presents to children. The kings are said to have visited Jesus on this night, and so children put straw or barley in their shoes for the travellers' weary camels. The shoes are left in doorways or on balconies, and in the morning the barley has gone, and has been replaced by sweets and presents.

★ In southern Italy the present-bringer is called *La Befana*. It is said that she met the three kings, who gave her the news about the birth of Jesus. Instead of immediately going to find him, she delayed until she had finished her work, and then lost her way when she finally set out. Now, tradition has it, *La Befana*

wanders the earth in search of the child from heaven, and leaves presents at every home in case he should be there. A similar legend can be heard in Russia about the kindly grandmother, *Baboushka*.

★ Christmas in Australia happens in the middle of summer. Nevertheless, most families still have traditional roast turkey followed by plum pudding for their Christmas dinner. Many Australians head for the coast at Christmas, so Christmas dinner may well be eaten on the beach. At Surfer's Paradise, Santa Claus usually arrives on water skis and wearing red bathing trunks!

★ On Christmas Eve in Britain and the United States, children—and many adults too—hang up Christmas stockings by their beds, or around the fireplace. Santa Claus or Father Christmas arrives by reindeer-drawn sleigh on the roof. He then climbs down the chimney, enjoys the food and drink left for him, and leaves, having filled the stockings with small toys, sweets, nuts and other goodies.

Father Christmas, with his white beard and red robes, brings the Christmas presents in many different parts of the world.

Stocking up for Christmas

These days very few people hang up their everyday socks and stockings for Santa Claus to fill. It's fun to make a special stocking for each individual member of the family.

You need:

Newspaper
Squared paper
Plain fabric or coloured felt
Needle
Thread
Scissors
Tape or ribbon
Braid or lace
Pieces of coloured felt
Sequins
Beads
Rubber-based adhesive

To make:

1 Decide how big you want your stocking to be. This of course depends how much you want to fit into it! Make a newspaper pattern of the basic shape, and use it as a template when cutting out your fabric.

2 Fold your fabric in half, and pin onto the newspaper template. Cut out shape. If using a sewing machine, personalize your stocking at this stage.

3 Placing right sides together, sew around all but the top edges. Turn over top edges and hem them, at the same time sewing in a loop of tape or ribbon for hanging up the stocking.

4 Turn stocking right side out (unless using felt) and decorate top edge with braid, lace or ribbon.

To personalize your stocking

★ Cut out felt letters to make the person's name and a felt shape for the motif you have chosen. Stick them in place with a rubber-based adhesive, and—for a really neat finish—stitch around the outside of each letter and shape.

★ Decorate felt shapes with sequins and beads if desired—for example: lights on the Christmas tree, buttons on the snowman.

Make a festive Mexican *Piñata*

You need:

Newspaper
Flour
Water
Medium balloon
Small toys and sweets
String or ribbon
Bright poster paint
Feathers or wool, fur and cotton wool
Sequins
Glitter
Glue

To make:

1 Tear several sheets of newspaper into narrow strips about 8cm long.

2 Make a thick paste of flour and water (or use wallpaper paste).

3 Blow up the balloon. Cover it with several layers of the paste-covered strips—criss-cross to give extra strength. Leave to dry between layers for about half an hour. Leave a hole at one end, big enough to push small sweets and toys inside. Allow to dry overnight in a warm place.

4 Burst balloon, and fill with small gifts and sweets. Paste a few strips over the hole to seal in the presents.

5 Decorate the *Piñata* as a bird or animal, with bright paint, feathers, sequins and glitter. Make two holes in one end and thread through string or ribbon to make a loop for hanging.

6 Hang up the *Piñata* and allow children to take it in turns to hit it with a stick, until it breaks open and the gifts pour out.

The crowning glory

What could be more fitting to top off your stocking than a golden crown, on a day when we celebrate the birth of the King of kings? These presents will be the crowning glory of Christmas morning, as they peep out of the top of bulging Christmas stockings.

You need:

Stiff gold card
Glue or stapler
Cotton wool
Fruit gums
Gold braid
Sequins

To make:

1 Find an excuse to measure around each child's head.

2 Make the crowns from stiff gold card and glue or staple them to the right size.

3 Decorate with glued-on cotton wool 'ermine', sparkling fruit-gum gems, gold braid or sequins.

Children in Mexico look forward at Christmas to the Piñata game.

The greatest gift of all

In countries where presents are placed under the Christmas tree before they are given, a child will often sneak into the room to peep at the presents, and look at the gift-tags. If theirs is the biggest present they will go away happy, if the smallest they will probably feel disappointed. Of course, appearances can be deceptive. In the smallest package may be hidden a musical box, or a first watch.

Appearances were deceptive when God gave the world the gift of his only son. The old masters' paintings show the baby bathed in a halo of soft light, but it is more likely that Jesus looked like any other newborn child. He didn't come wrapped in silk and gold, but in strips of cloth, and lying in an animal's feeding trough. The greatest gift ever given was not to be recognized by the wrapping; Jesus' true identity was to be found by looking beyond appearances.

Presents with taste

Edible presents are always welcome at Christmas, and a well-presented box of home-made sweets or chocolates has twice the appeal of shop-bought ones. After all, you're giving your time and culinary talent as well as your money.

Rich chocolate truffles

You need:
75g (3oz) plain chocolate
50g (2oz) ground almonds
50g (2oz) caster sugar
2tbs amaretto, rum or brandy (optional)
Chocolate vermicelli or drinking chocolate
Small paper cake cases

To make:

1 Melt chocolate gently in a bowl placed over a saucepan of hot water, add ground almonds, sugar and amaretto, rum or brandy.

2 Shape into small balls, roll in vermicelli or drinking chocolate, and put in small paper cake cases.

3 The truffles will keep in a plastic container in the fridge for up to one month. Present in a box covered with Christmas paper and lined with a doily, or buy a gift box or little decorative carrier for them.

Chocolate chip cookies

Like sweets, crumbly home-made biscuits and cookies are a welcome addition to anyone's Christmas supplies. If you want to make them in advance, here is a recipe for cookies which can be frozen in a rigid container and kept for several weeks. Thaw for 10–15 minutes at room temperature before unpacking.

You need:
200g (7oz) flour
1/2 tsp baking powder
Pinch of salt
110g (4oz) butter
110g (4oz) caster sugar
2tbs golden syrup
1 egg, lightly beaten
110g (4oz) chocolate polka dots, or plain chocolate cut into small chips

To make:

1 Preheat oven to 190°C/375°F/Gas 5.

2 Cream together butter, sugar and syrup until light and fluffy. Beat in the egg.

3 Sift dry ingredients and stir in together with chocolate pieces.

4 Place teaspoonfuls of mixture on greased baking sheets, separating to allow for spreading, and bake for 12–15 minutes. Cool on a wire rack.

5 Wrap cookies carefully in cellophane and

decorate with ribbon, or pack them into a decorative biscuit tin so that there will be something left of your gift when Christmas comes!

But what if all your friends are on a diet and would run a mile from a box of chocolates? Present them with a jar of home-made relish or pickled onions, to spice up their cold Christmas meat.

Spiced apple chutney

You need:

225g (8oz) cooking apples (peeled, cored and
  roughly diced)
110g (4oz) sultanas
110g (4oz) dates (stoned and chopped)
110g (4oz) dried apricots (chopped)
110g (4oz) soft brown sugar
150ml (1/4 pt) malt vinegar
1/4 tsp hot chilli powder
1/2 tsp mixed spice
1/4 tsp salt
Glass jars
Plastic film

To make:

1 Place all the ingredients in a heavy saucepan. Simmer gently for 15 minutes or until thick and pulpy.

2 Leave to cool, then spoon into sterilized glass jars.

Pickling made simple

You need:

Pickling onions (shallots)
Salt
Water
Malt vinegar

To make:

1 Soak pickling onions (shallots), skins and all, in cold water for several hours. This makes it easier to peel them.

2 Remove skins, and trim top and bottom, leaving the root ends until last to minimize watering eyes.

3 Cover onions with a strong salt solution and leave overnight. Rinse well and pack tightly into glass jars. Cover with malt pickling vinegar and seal. Store for at least two weeks before eating.

Tips for tops

★ Either use jars with glass stoppers or make sure that metal tops are protected from the corrosive vinegar by a layer of plastic film.

★ Add a festive touch by decorating jar tops with circles of Christmas fabric or wrapping paper, secured by an elastic band. Decorate with artificial holly, ribbon or tinsel and a 'Home made for . . .' label.

THE MAKING OF SANTA CLAUS

How did the good fourth-century bishop, St Nicholas, become the jolly red-suited Santa Claus, also known as Father Christmas?

Greenland, Lapland, the North Pole—nobody knows for sure where Santa Claus lives, but children the world over look forward to the coming of the jolly old man in a red suit, with a sack of presents on his back.

The origins of Santa Claus date back to the fourth century and St Nicholas, Archbishop of Myra. Many stories are told about the kind bishop, who became the patron saint of children. He is said once to have travelled to the West, to deliver fruit and honey cakes to hungry children. In another story, he provided dowries of gold for the three daughters of a poor nobleman. One of the bags of gold dropped down the chimney and

This nineteenth-century Dutch painting shows St Nicholas in his bishop's robes holding presents for the children.

landed in a stocking hung up to dry—and that's why some countries have Christmas stockings.

When the Church chose 6 December as St Nicholas' Day, it became the custom for someone dressed as St Nicholas to visit children. Good children were rewarded with presents, and bad children threatened with punishment (though it is doubtful whether the original St Nicholas would have subscribed to this attitude!) In countries such as Holland, Germany and Belgium, the tradition of St Nicholas' Day is still very much alive.

After the Reformation, the whole idea of saints went out of favour in Protestant countries. In England, St Nicholas merged with the pagan character of Old Christmas in the medieval entertainments called mummers' plays.

Meanwhile, Dutch settlers in America took the tradition of St Nicholas with them. The custom of leaving out your shoes for *Sinterklaas* soon spread across the country.

In 1822 Dr Clement Clarke Moore, a professor in New York, wrote a poem for his children, 'A Visit from St Nicholas'. It was published in *The Troy Sentinel*, and overnight changed the kindly bishop into the Santa Claus we know today.

'His eyes how they twinkled! His dimples how merry!
His cheeks were like roses, his nose like a cherry.
His droll little mouth was drawn up like a bow,
And the beard on his chin was as white as the snow'

Magazine illustrators did the rest, adding the final touches to the jovial character in a red suit, flying across the rooftops in a reindeer-drawn sleigh. Santa Claus recrossed the Atlantic and merged with Old Christmas to become Father Christmas in England; nowadays the names are interchangeable.

Today a town in America called Santa Claus receives over three million letters a year from children—and there are many others, sent to Greenland, Lapland and the North Pole. From being a bishop in fourth-century Turkey, St Nicholas has come a long way.

WE THREE KINGS

We three kings of Orient are;
Bearing gifts we traverse afar
Field and fountain, moor and mountain,
Following yonder star:
  O star of wonder, star of night,
  Star with royal beauty bright,
  Westward leading, still proceeding,
  Guide us to thy perfect light.

Born a King on Bethlehem plain
Gold I bring to crown him again;
King for ever, ceasing never
Over us all to reign:

Frankincense to offer have I,
Incense owns a deity nigh;
Prayer and praising, all men raising,
Worship him, God most high:

Myrrh is mine; its bitter perfume
Breathes a life of gathering gloom;
Sorrowing, sighing, bleeding, dying
Sealed in the stone-cold tomb:

JOHN HENRY HOPKINS (1820–91)

ROOM AT THE INN?

FEASTS FOR THE FESTIVAL

Food for thought

In every culture where Christmas is celebrated, it is traditionally a time for feasting. In some countries, the joy of feasting is highlighted by a previous time of fasting! The Italians treat the day before Christmas as a fast day, and in Romania they feast until the end of the year, and then fast for the first days of the New Year.

Some of the Christmas dishes eaten around the world are symbolic, with a religious significance which adds to the meaning of the festival. Others simply represent the saving of the best and richest produce of the year for a special time with friends and family. The

sharing of a meal is a time-honoured ritual, which can break down barriers between people and help to develop the spirit of warmth and friendship which is an essential part of Christmas.

Now that the time has come wherein
Our Saviour Christ was born,
The larder's full of beef and pork,
The granaries full of corn.
As God hath plenty to thee sent,
Take comfort of thy labours,
And let it never thee repent
To feed thy needy neighbours.

TRADITIONAL ENGLISH

" 'Never again!' I said last Christmas. There was father asleep, trussed up in front of the telly like an overstuffed turkey, the children up to their elbows in Christmas pudding, looking for money, and Uncle Hal pickling himself slowly in port. I love food, but this year it's not going to take over so much that I miss out on the rest of Christmas.

If you ask me, I sympathize with the Innkeeper, the one who turned Joseph and Mary away. You can just see him, sleeves rolled up, red-faced and puffing, surrounded by impatient guests, and bellowing orders to the chef in the kitchen. A servant interrupts to say there's a man and a pregnant woman outside, asking for a room.

'Room?' he says, 'Look around you, I've got fifty hungry guests howling for their evening meal. Tell them there is no room.' And he bustles back to the food and drink, unaware that he just missed God's Son coming to his house."

Every part of Europe has its own dishes that symbolize Christmas, and trying some of them out allows us to discover the richness of different festive traditions.

Main dishes from around Europe

In Germany, traditional food includes roast pork or goose with red cabbage, and game such as hare, venison and pheasant. On Christmas Eve, the main dish in many homes is a fish one, such as pickled herring.

Housewife's herring

You need:

8 herring fillets, approx 400g (1 lb) each
2tbs wine vinegar
2tbs sugar
2 medium apples
2 medium onions
1 large gherkin (dill pickle)
250ml (1/2 pint) sour cream

To make:

1 Wash herrings. If too salty, soak in water for 1–2 hours, changing water frequently.

2 Mix together wine vinegar and sugar and pour over herrings laid in a flat dish. Leave covered for 2 hours to marinate.

3 Peel apples and onions. Cut them, and the gherkins, into thin slices.

4 Lay apples, onions and gherkins in layers on top of the herrings. Pour over sour cream.

5 Cover and leave for one hour in the fridge.

6 Serve with small new potatoes and a beetroot salad.

In Scandinavia, the Christmas meal, served on Christmas Eve, is most often roast pork with a crisp crackling, or perhaps goose or duck. On Christmas Day itself, an enormous *smörgasbord* (or cold table) is laid out at lunchtime, with numerous dishes of cold meat, pickled fish, salads and cheeses. This recipe for pork can be served hot or cold on either of these occasions.

Rolled loin of pork with prune and apple stuffing

(SERVES 6–8)

You need:

1 loin of pork, 1.35–1.6 kg (3–3^1/$_2$ lb) boned weight
Salt and pepper
8 or 9 no-need-to-soak dried prunes
^{1}/$_2$ Granny Smith apple, cored and chopped
Oil for brushing

To make:

1 Place unrolled pork, skin side down, on a chopping board.

2 Season meat with salt and pepper, and arrange chopped apple and prunes evenly down the centre. Re-roll and tie securely with string.

3 Score rind with a sharp knife. Brush with a little oil and sprinkle with salt to ensure crisp crackling.

4 Roast at 425° F/220° C/Gas 7 for 30 minutes, then at 375° F/190° C/Gas 5 for a further 30 minutes per pound of meat.

5 Serve hot or cold.

In France, a rich Christmas meal called the **Réveillon** is traditionally served on Christmas Eve. This often includes pâté and shellfish as well as roast game, turkey or goose. The meal should always contain a dish using black pudding, as does this goose recipe from Normandy.

You will find endless advice on cooking a Christmas turkey in recipe books and magazines. So here are some ideas for stuffings and sauces, to complement the crowning glory of the table at a traditional British Christmas dinner.

Oie à la Normande

(SERVES 6–8)

You need:

1 goose, approximately 4$\frac{1}{2}$ kg (10lb)
450g (1lb) black pudding
1 crushed garlic clove
2 large dessert apples, peeled and grated
65ml (2$\frac{1}{2}$ fl oz) port
Salt and pepper

To make:

1 Pound the skinned black pudding with garlic and goose liver until smooth.

2 Blend in the apples, and bind the stuffing with the port. Stuff the goose with this mixture.

3 Prick skin all over with a skewer and rub with salt and pepper. Cover goose with foil and roast at 400° F/220° C/Gas 6 for 15 minutes to the pound plus 15 minutes.

4 Drain the fat from the pan after 1 hour, and pour 100ml (4fl oz) cold water over the goose.

5 30 minutes before cooking is complete, remove foil and baste the goose every 10 minutes with the juices.

6 Serve on a thick bed of unsweetened apple purée, decorated with polished red apples.

In Great Britain, the main celebration meal may be eaten on Christmas Eve in some families, but is more often on Christmas Day itself. Although roast pork, goose and even roast beef are often eaten, the now internationally accepted roast turkey appears as the centrepiece on most tables.

Traditional stuffing

(SUFFICIENT FOR 6.3 KG (14LB) TURKEY)

You need:

1 onion
75g (3oz) butter
25g (1oz) fresh root ginger
50g (2oz) walnut pieces
675g (1$\frac{1}{2}$ lbs) pork sausage-meat
150g (6oz) fresh breadcrumbs
4tbs chopped parsley
Salt and pepper

To make:

1 Finely chop onion and fry in 25g (1oz) butter until softened but not browned. Cool.

2 Peel and grate ginger. Chop walnuts. Place in a bowl with sausage-meat, breadcrumbs, parsley and plenty of salt and pepper. Mix well.

3 Spoon half of the stuffing into the neck end of the turkey. Do not pack too tightly. Fold the neck flap under the turkey. Truss with string.

4 Shape remaining stuffing into about 40 walnut-sized balls and place in a greased roasting tin. Cook in the oven for the final 20 minutes of the turkey's cooking time.

Chestnut stuffing

(SUFFICIENT FOR 6.3 KG (14LB) TURKEY)

You need:

450g (1lb) frozen, tinned or prepared fresh chestnuts
225g (8oz) streaky bacon, chopped

15g (1/2 oz) butter
100g (4oz) fresh breadcrumbs
1 egg, beaten
6tbs chopped parsley

To make:

1 Chop chestnuts coarsely.

2 Fry bacon over gentle heat in a non-stick pan until fat begins to ooze. Increase heat, add chestnuts and fry quickly until bacon is crisp and nuts are beginning to colour. Lift out with a slotted spoon, transfer to a mixing bowl.

3 Add butter to the pan with the bacon fat. Allow to melt. Add breadcrumbs and fry until brown. Transfer to bowl.

4 Add remaining ingredients, season with salt and freshly-ground black pepper. Mix well. Cool, then use to stuff turkey, as described above.

Cranberry sauce

(MAKES 300ML (1/4 PINT))

You need:

75ml (3fl oz) water
250g (8oz) cranberries
75g (3oz) sugar

To make:

1 Place water and cranberries in a small sauce-pan, bring to the boil, cook gently until skins pop.

2 Add sugar and dissolve, then cook for 3 minutes. Allow to cool.

3 Serve in a dish to accompany roast meats.

Bread sauce

(SERVES 8)

You need:

1 onion
4 cloves
600ml (1 pint) milk
1 blade of mace or 1/2 tsp ground nutmeg
1 bay leaf
100g (4oz) fresh white breadcrumbs
25g (1oz) butter
Salt and pepper

To make:

1 Peel the onion, and spike it with the cloves.

2 Put into a saucepan with the milk, mace and bay leaf. Bring slowly to the boil.

3 Remove from heat, cover and leave to infuse for 30 minutes.

4 Discard onion, mace and bay leaf. Add breadcrumbs, salt and pepper to milk. Bring to the boil, stirring until very thick.

5 Add the butter and stir until melted. Spoon into a warmed sauce boat and grind plenty of black pepper over it. Serve hot as an accompaniment to roast turkey.

Here is a special festive recipe for those who prefer a meatless alternative to the traditional centrepiece of the Christmas meal.

Christmas pie

(SERVES 8)

You need for the pastry:

150g (6oz) self-raising wholemeal flour
150g (6oz) plain flour
1/4 tsp salt
275g (9oz) margarine

For the sauce:

2 vegetable stock cubes
1 packet (10 strands) saffron (or 1tsp each
  ground cumin and coriander)
100g (4oz) butter
100g (4oz) plain flour
150ml (1/4 pint) dry white wine

To make:

1 Put flour and salt into a large bowl.

2 Cut fat into tiny cubes. Add to bowl and mix well.

For the filling:

225g (8oz) whole chestnuts
100g (4oz) ready-to-eat dried apricots
410g (14oz) canned chick peas
3tbs plain flour
3tbsp oil
3 heads of fennel
500g (1lb) courgettes
500g (1lb) leeks
375g (12oz) broccoli
250g (8oz) swede
250g (8oz) broad beans

3 Stir in 200ml (7fl oz) cold water. Mix to a soft dough with a knife.

4 Knead lightly. Roll out to a rectangle 13cm x 36cm (5in. x 14in.).

5 Fold top third of pastry over centre of pastry. Fold bottom third of pastry up over first fold. Wrap in polythene and chill for 30 minutes.

6 Rotate pastry so that folded edges are vertical. Roll to same size as before and repeat folding. Repeat process one more time. Cover with plastic and chill while preparing filling.

7 Make a cross cut in the base of each chestnut. Place in a bowl, cover with boiling water, leave 5 minutes. Drain and peel off skins. Chop or process chestnuts, apricots and drained chick peas. Mix together with plenty of seasoning.

8 Shape mixture into small balls and roll in flour. Fry in hot oil until evenly brown. Drain well and keep to one side.

9 Thinly slice fennel, reserving green feathery tops. Thickly slice courgettes and leeks; trim broccoli. Peel and finely dice swede. Blanch swede in boiling lightly salted water for 5 minutes, and remaining vegetables for 2 minutes. Drain, rinse under cold water. Reserve 1 litre (2 pints) vegetable water for sauce.

10 Arrange stuffing balls, vegetables and broad beans in a large 2.5 litre (5 pint) pie dish. Chop feathery fennel and sprinkle over.

11 Dissolve vegetable stock cubes in reserved hot vegetable water. Crush saffron, add to stock and leave to infuse for at least 30 minutes.

12 Pre-heat oven to 220°C/425°F/Gas 7.

13 Melt butter in a large saucepan. Stir in flour and cook for 1 minute. Gradually add saffron stock, stirring well until smooth. Add wine and plenty of seasoning. Bring to the boil. Pour three-quarters of the sauce over vegetables in pie dish, reserving the rest to serve separately.

14 Top pie with pastry lid. Flute pie edge with the back of a knife. Brush with beaten egg. Cut trimmings into thin strips and arrange on pie to decorate.

15 Cook for 35 minutes until golden brown. Serve hot with reserved sauce, and the following vegetable dishes.

Sesame parsnips

(SERVES 8)

You need:

1.25kg (2¹/₂ lb) small parsnips
6tbs vegetable oil
6tbs sesame seeds

To make:

Peel parsnips. Heat oil in large roasting tin in the oven. Add parsnips, toss in oil. Sprinkle sesame seeds over. Roast at 220°C/425°F/Gas 7 for 1 hour on lower shelf.

Glazed carrots

(SERVES 8)

You need:

500g (1lb) carrots
30g (1oz) margarine or butter
2tsp soft brown sugar

To make:

Cut carrots into thin sticks. Cook in boiling salted water about 5 minutes until tender, drain. Add margarine and soft brown sugar, toss over low heat to form a glaze. Serve sprinkled with chopped parsley.

The plum pudding boiled in a cloth bag, round and fat with a sprig of holly on the top, so beloved of Christmas card designers, is actually quite a late entry in the Christmas pudding stakes. The original was a thick porridge made with meat, wine, fruit juice, raisins, spices and dried plums—hence the name plum pudding. It was thickened even further with brown bread, and eaten with a spoon. A more palatable alternative today might be this Danish Christmas 'porridge'. In times past this was served at the beginning of the meal and would hide a large whole almond—whoever found it won a small prize, such as a marzipan pig!

Christmas-time creamed rice with almonds

(SERVES 6)

You need:

600ml (1 pint) milk
110g (4oz) round-grain pudding rice
Vanilla pod
60g (2oz) blanched almonds, chopped
30g (1oz) caster sugar
1tbs cherry brandy (optional)
'Silver' or 'gold' almonds to decorate

To make:

1 Bring the milk to the boil in a heavy-based pan. Add the rice and vanilla pod. Cook, stirring, for 5 minutes, then cover and simmer very gently for 25 minutes, stirring occasionally.

2 Remove the vanilla pod and leave to cool. Stir in the almonds, sugar and cherry brandy.

3 Lightly whip the cream and fold into the rice. Serve in a pretty bowl chilled and decorated with the almonds. Especially good with stewed fruit.

In Britain, the modern descendant of the rich plum porridge is a steamed pudding bursting with dried fruit, often made long before Christmas or even saved from the previous year! Some people still make their pudding on 'Stir-up Sunday', the last Sunday before Advent, so called because the prayer for that Sunday in the Anglican Book of Common Prayer begins:

'Stir up, we beseech Thee, O Lord, the wills of Thy faithful people …'

In some households everyone has a turn at stirring the pudding, and in just a few homes a silver coin is still hidden in the pudding by the youngest member of the family—if you do this, wrap it in foil, as it makes it less likely that it will be swallowed or break somebody's tooth!

Traditional British Christmas pudding

You need:

250g (9oz) currants
250g (9oz) raisins
225g (8oz) sultanas
50g (2oz) glacé cherries, chopped
50g (2oz) whole candied citrus peel, chopped
75g (3oz) self-raising flour
1tbs mixed spice
75g (3oz) fresh brown breadcrumbs
50g (2oz) soft dark brown sugar
100g (4oz) shredded suet
1 apple, peeled, cored and grated
1 lemon, grated rind and juice
1 orange, grated rind and juice
50g (2oz) whole almonds, chopped
2 eggs, beaten
3tbs brandy
3tbs light ale

To make:

1 Mix all ingredients together, and press down into a 1.25 litre (2½ pint) greased pudding basin.

2 Cover top with greaseproof paper and aluminium foil, folding in a pleat across the centre and securing with string.

3 Steam in a covered saucepan of gently boiling water for 3 hours, making sure that the saucepan does not boil dry.

4 Serve with cream or brandy butter. If made in advance this pudding will keep for months; simply steam for a further hour to re-heat.

We wish you a merry Christmas,
We wish you a merry Christmas,
We wish you a merry Christmas,
And a happy New Year!
   Glad tidings we bring
   To you and your kin;
   We wish you a merry Christmas,
   And a happy New Year!

We all want some figgy pudding,
We all want some figgy pudding,
We all want some figgy pudding,
So send some out here!

And we won't go until we've got some,
We won't go until we've got some,
We won't go until we've got some,
So send some out here!

TRADITIONAL ENGLISH

Sometimes at the end of a rich Christmas meal you cannot face a heavy pudding. This wonderfully light British dessert is a good alternative.

Angel food pudding

(SERVES 4)

You need:

3 eggs, separated
75g (3oz) caster sugar
Juice of 1 lemon
2tbs dry white wine
Grated rind of ½ lemon
150ml (¼ pt) whipped double cream
Chocolate vermicelli

To make:

1 Beat the egg yolks and sugar together until creamy, then gradually add the lemon juice, wine and lemon rind.

2 Pour into a thick-based pan and heat gently, stirring continuously until it thickens. Be careful not to overheat or it will curdle. Allow to cool.

3 Whisk the egg whites stiffly and fold into the mixture.

4 Pile into individual glasses and chill before serving. Decorate with whipped cream and chocolate vermicelli.

The British Christmas pudding has a long history. At one time it was known as 'bag pudding' because it was wrapped in a bag for steaming.

Christmas cookies

Biscuits are a particular feature of Christmas fare throughout Europe. In Denmark, guests are traditionally not allowed to leave a house without sampling their host's Christmas biscuits. This custom dates back to medieval times when poor people, making their rounds before Christmas, would be given something to eat, to ensure that they would not take Christmas away with them as they left.

Finnish shortbread

(MAKES 65)

This is similar to the biscuit traditionally made and eaten in Scotland at Hogmanay (the coming of the New Year). It is light and almond-flavoured.

You need:

170g (6oz) butter, chilled and diced
230g (8oz) self-raising flour
100g (4oz) caster sugar
A few drops of almond essence
1 egg white, size 3, lightly beaten
Granulated sugar and a few chopped almonds for sprinkling

To make:

1 Rub the butter into the flour until the mixture resembles fine crumbs. Stir in the sugar and almond essence, then knead the mixture together to form a smooth dough. Wrap and chill for about an hour.

2 On a floured work surface, roll out the dough about 6mm (1/4 in) thick. Brush with egg white and sprinkle with granulated sugar. Scatter the almonds over the dough, pressing gently so they stick to it.

3 Cut into fingers about 5cm x 2cm (2in x 3/4 in) and transfer to greased baking trays. Chill for 15–20 minutes before baking.

4 Bake the chilled biscuits for 10–12 minutes at 220°C/425°F/Gas 7 until barely golden. Cool for a few minutes then transfer to a wire rack. Store in an airtight container or freezer for up to a month.

Christmas shapes can be made from almost any basic biscuit dough. Iced, or sprinkled with sugar, they make attractive decorations for your tree. Some, like these Christmas stars from Germany, will quickly go soft and spoil, so store them carefully and bring out a few at a time.

Christmas stars

You need:

1 egg white
175g (6oz) caster sugar
150g (5oz) ground almonds
2tsp ground cinnamon
1 pinch ground cloves
Finely grated rind of 1/2 lemon

For the icing:
1 egg white
100g (4oz) icing sugar
Squeeze of lemon juice
Coloured sugar strands or hundreds and thousands

To make:

1 Beat the egg white with all but 2tbs of the caster sugar until thick and white. Beat in ground almonds, cinnamon and lemon rind. Chill mixture for 1 hour.

2 Sprinkle half of remaining caster sugar onto a pastry board. Flatten the chilled dough mixture onto the board, then sprinkle on the remaining sugar. Roll out very thinly, then cut into stars.

3 Place on greased baking sheets and bake in a fairly hot oven: 190°C/375°F/Gas 5, for 10–15 minutes, or until they have risen slightly and are pale brown. Cool on wire rack.

4 Beat the egg white, icing sugar and lemon juice together until very thick. Spread thickly on biscuits, and dust with sugar strands or hundreds and thousands.

Christmas crumbs

What is known in Britain as Christmas cake was originally baked in celebration of Epiphany or Twelfth Night, when the Magi, or wise men, are traditionally said to have arrived in Bethlehem to visit the child Jesus. Early recipes dating from the seventeenth century use massive quantities, demanding 20 eggs, 4lbs currants and 2lbs butter. In Holland they still bake Twelfth Night cake, and hide a dried bean in it. The person finding the bean becomes 'King' or 'Queen' for the day!

In Britain, Christmas cake appears in every home. Often it is baked well before Christmas, covered in marzipan and iced with white icing. A paper or ribbon band is wrapped around it and the top is decorated with plastic or plaster Christmas figures.

Christmas cake

(18CM (7IN) SQUARE OR 20CM (8IN) ROUND)

You need:

225g (8oz) butter
225g (8oz) dark brown sugar
325g (12oz) plain flour
2tsp ground mixed spice
1tsp ground cinnamon
1/4 tsp ground nutmeg
5 eggs
100g (4oz) glacé cherries
75g (3oz) chopped mixed nuts
100g (4oz) mixed peel
275g (10oz) sultanas
275g (10oz) currants
275g (10oz) raisins
900g (2lb) marzipan for covering

For decoration icing:
2 egg whites
2 rounded tbs liquid glucose
900g (2lb) icing sugar
Food colours if required

To make:

1 Preheat oven to 275°F/140°C/Gas 1.

2 Grease and line base of cake tin.

3 Cream together butter and sugar. Sift flour with spices. Gradually beat eggs into creamed mixture, adding a little flour to prevent curdling. Stir in rest of flour.

4 Cut up cherries. Add with nuts, peel and dried fruit. Fill tin and level.

5 Cook for $3^1/_2$ to $3^3/_4$ hours, until a skewer inserted into the centre of the cake comes out clean. Leave to cool in tin.

6 Wrap in foil until needed. The flavour of this cake matures with keeping.

7 Brush with apricot jam and cover with marzipan before decorating.

8 Mix together egg whites, reserving a little, and liquid glucose. Gradually beat in sifted icing sugar. If mixture becomes too stiff knead by hand. Store in polythene bag until needed.

9 Roll, mould and model icing like clay, to cut 2-D shapes and letters out of it, or make 3-D models and figures. Stick finished shapes onto the cake with reserved egg white.

10 Once the decoration icing is dry, paint or write on it with food colouring pens or a paintbrush.

In the days before split-level cookers and fan-assisted ovens, it was important to get a good hot fire going in the kitchen, to roast meat and toast toes! So a huge log was selected and dragged indoors. Whether or not you have the luxury of an open fire, you can enjoy this traditional French yule log. You can also replace the chestnut filling with chocolate butter cream, to please the children and keep the cost down.

Bûche de Noël aux marrons

You need:

3 eggs
75g (3oz) caster sugar
50g (2oz) self-raising flour
2tsp cocoa
Pinch of salt

For the filling:

100g (4oz) sweet chestnut purée
50ml (2fl oz) dark rum (optional)
425ml (15fl oz) whipping cream
2tbs caster sugar

To make:

1 Grease and line a Swiss roll tin.

2 Whisk eggs and sugar until thick and fluffy.

3 Sift in the flour and gently stir in the cocoa.

4 Spread mixture evenly over tin. Bake for 10 minutes at 200° C/400° F/Gas 6.

5 Cool slightly, turn out onto greaseproof paper. Trim the ends and roll carefully with the sheet of paper. Leave to cool.

6 Combine chestnut pureé with rum (if not using rum, add same quantity of water).

7 Stir in 150ml (5fl oz) of the cream and set aside. Lightly whip remainder of cream with sugar and fold into purée with a spoon.

8 To assemble, peel off greaseproof paper and spread sponge with two-thirds of chestnut cream. Roll up from the short end and place on serving plate. Cover with remaining chestnut cream and create log effect with a fork.

Tosca cake

(MAKES ONE 21.5CM ($8^1/_2$ IN) CAKE)

This Danish cake for Christmas has a deliciously nutty flavour.

You need:

100g (4oz) unsalted butter
100g (4oz) caster sugar
Grated rind of one lemon
2 eggs, beaten
25g (1oz) ground almonds
70g ($2^1/_2$ oz) plain flour
$1/_2$ tsp baking powder

For the topping:

85g (3oz) unsalted butter
100g (4oz) chopped almonds
1tbsp plain flour
2tsp single cream

To make:

1 Grease and base-line tin.

2 Cream butter with sugar and lemon rind until light and fluffy. Gradually beat in eggs.

3 Sift ground almonds, flour and baking powder and carefully fold into mixture with a metal spoon.

4 Spoon mixture into prepared tin and smooth surface. Bake for 25–30 minutes at 180°C/350°F/ Gas 4 until cake is firm to the touch.

5 Melt the butter, stir in remaining ingredients and bring to the boil. Simmer for 3–5 minutes, stirring constantly, until mixture has thickened.

6 Pour the topping onto the cake and return to oven. Cook for a further 10 minutes until topping is golden brown.

7 Cool slightly in the tin before cooling on a wire rack. Store in an airtight container and eat within 5 days.

Snow white chocolate cake

An American cake, this looks very bright and white on a Christmas tea-table, but gives the surprise of a rich, dark, chocolatey inside when it is cut.

You need:

100g (4oz) cocoa
375ml (3/4 pint) boiling water
200g (8oz) butter (softened)
400g (15oz) sugar
400g (15oz) plain flour
2tsp bicarbonate of soda
1/2 tsp baking powder
4 eggs (beaten)

For the frosting:

300g (12oz) caster sugar
2 eggs whites
1/4 tsp cream of tartar
Edible silver balls to decorate

To make:

1 Mix cocoa and boiling water until smooth. Leave to cool.

2 Cream butter and sugar until light and fluffy.

3 Sift flour, bicarbonate of soda and baking powder together. Gradually beat in eggs, with a little flour, beating well.

4 Fold in cocoa mixture alternately with remaining flour mixture.

5 Pour mixture into a greased, base-lined, deep 19cm (7½in) round tin. Cook for 1¼ hours at 180°C/350°F/Gas 4.

6 Cool on a wire rack turned upside down with tin in place.

7 Turn out cake. Cut into three layers and put bottom layer on a round cake board.

8 Put sugar, egg whites and cream of tartar for frosting in a large bowl over a pan of gently boiling water and whisk until smooth. Continue whisking until mixture forms stiff peaks, about 8–10 minutes.

9 Sandwich cake layers together with a little frosting. Quickly spoon remaining frosting over cake swirling into peaks with a knife.

10 Press silver balls into frosting peaks. Store in airtight container for up to 1 week.

Give us this day our Christmas bread

In Germany, an essential part of Christmas celebrations is the Christstollen, a rich fruit bread eaten throughout the whole of the festival from Christmas Eve onwards. The folding of the dough just before baking represents the swaddling of the Christ child in his bands. In many households, so many Stollen are prepared that they have to be taken to the local baker to be baked in his oven. There are many regional and family variations on the recipe but this one from Dresden is widely regarded as a favourite.

Dresdner Christollen

(MAKES 2)

You need:

60g (2½ oz) raisins
60g (2½ oz) currants
150g (5oz) mixed peel
40g (1½ oz) chopped angelica
75g (3oz) glacé cherries
50g (2oz) flaked almonds
16ml (4tbs) rum
45ml (3tbs) warm water
40g (1½ oz) fresh yeast
175g (6oz) caster sugar
150ml (¼ pint) tepid milk

675g (1lb 8oz) strong plain flour
1/2 tsp salt
1/2 tsp almond essence
1tbs grated lemon rind
2 eggs, beaten
100g (4oz) unsalted butter
50g (2oz) salted butter
75g (3oz) icing sugar

To make:

1 Mix first 6 ingredients with rum and soak for 1 hour.

2 Mix 1tsp caster sugar with warm water and fresh yeast. Stir in 100g (4oz) sugar and tepid milk. Leave to stand in a warm place 10 minutes.

3 Sift flour and salt into bowl and stir in almond essence, grated lemon rind, beaten egg and yeast liquid. Beat in unsalted butter which has been cut into small cubes.

4 Knead on floured surface until smooth. Knead in fruit mixture.

5 Place in a greased polythene bag and leave in a warm place until dough has doubled in size.

6 Set oven at 190°C/375°F/Gas 5. Grease 2 baking sheets.

7 Divide dough in half, and roll each piece to a 30.5cm x 20.5cm (12in x 8in) oblong. Melt the remaining salted butter and brush half of it over the dough. Sprinkle with remaining caster sugar.

8 Fold one of the long sides of the dough to the centre. Then bring the other side over it, overlapping by about 2.5cm (1 in). Repeat with other piece of dough.

9 Place each piece on a baking sheet, and brush with the reserved salted butter. Leave to stand in a warm place for 20 minutes. Bake for 40 minutes until firm and golden. Dredge with icing sugar, before serving in slices spread with butter.

Christmas star loaf

Almost any bread dough can be used to make this attractive loaf, which is shaped like the star which guided the Wise Men to Bethlehem. As the finished result is very decorative, it could also be used as part of a Christmas display at home, in school or in church. The plaiting needs a bit of practice, so try it out with thick wool, string or, ideally, children's play dough before you make the loaf.

1 Make up any rich bread dough recipe, using 675g–1kg (1½–2lb) flour. After the dough has risen to double size for the first time, divide into 12 equal parts and roll each part into a rope of finger thickness.

2 Group the ropes into 3 lots of 4, plaiting each group up to halfway along their length.

3 Take each plait and divide the remaining four ends into 2 lots of 2, folding them back down the sides of the plait. Place the 3 plaits on a greased baking sheet to form 3 points of a star, with the free end facing outwards.

4 Taking 2 strands from each neighbouring group, plait a new strand of 4, working towards the outside of the star. Continue in this way until all the strands are plaited.

5 Allow to rest in a warm place again briefly, brush with egg yolk and bake at 200°C/400°F/Gas 6 for 20 minutes or until golden.

CHRISTMAS CHEERS!

Many people want to avoid alcoholic drinks at Christmas time. Here are lots of exciting alternatives for your Christmas party or for a cosy evening by the fire. So, propose a toast to Christmas . . . and drink as much as you like!

Frosty favourites

Dip the rims of some glasses first into water and then into sugar. Put to chill until your guests arrive, and then fill with one of these refreshing party favourites from around the world.

White Christmas

(CARIBBEAN, SERVES 6)

You need:

500ml (1 pint) milk
4tbs desiccated coconut
1 ripe mango
1 banana
6 ice cubes

To make:

1 Heat milk to boiling with half the coconut. Leave to cool for 10 minutes. Toast remaining coconut.

2 Put mango, flat side down, on a board. Cut round through to stone, pull apart halves. Peel and slice.

3 Peel and slice banana. Process or liquidize half the banana, half the mango and the coconut milk and ice cubes.

4 Cut remaining banana slices and mango into small pieces, coat banana with toasted coconut. Thread on cocktail sticks.

5 Serve cocktail in tall glasses, topped with the fruit sticks and a cocktail stirrer.

Chocolate frappé

(FRANCE, SERVES 4)

You need:

2 heaped tbs drinking chocolate
3tbs boiling water
750ml (1½ pints) chilled milk
2tbs whipped fresh double cream
Crushed ice

To make:

1 Cover base of four glasses with crushed ice.

2 Mix drinking chocolate with water to a smooth liquid.

3 Whisk in milk.

4 Serve in glasses topped with cream.

Podina ka sharbat

(INDIA, SERVES 4–6)

You need:

A good handful of fresh mint leaves
½ tsp cinnamon
½ tsp nutmeg
500ml (1 pint) boiling water
1 lemon
100g (4oz) sugar
6 cloves
6 cardamoms

To make:

1 Chop mint leaves finely.

2 Place in saucepan, pour boiling water over them. Bring to boil, then reduce to a gentle simmer.

3 Add sugar, cloves, cardamoms, cinnamon and nutmeg. Simmer for 10 minutes then squeeze the juice of a lemon into a pan.

4 Increase heat and boil quickly for 15 minutes to reduce amount of liquid.

5 Remove from heat and strain sharbat through a fine sieve. Pour into jug and refrigerate.

6 Serve diluted half-and-half with iced water and plenty of ice.

Winter warmers

If your idea of a Christmas drink is to put your hands around a warm mug on a cold frosty night, then these ideas will be more to your taste.

Marshmallow floats

(SERVES 4)

You need:

500ml (1 pint) milk
2tbs drinking chocolate
8 marshmallows

To make:

1 Bring milk up to boil.

2 Remove from heat and whisk in drinking chocolate.

3 Serve in 4 cups, with 2 marshmallows floated in each.

Red fruit punch

(SERVES 4)

You need:

500ml (1 pint) red grape juice
125ml (¼ pint) apple juice
2.5cm (1 in) cinnamon stick
2tbs clear honey (less if fruit juice is sweetened)

To make:

Mix all ingredients and cook on a medium heat until hot, stirring occasionally. Serve in warmed glasses.

Almond flip

(SERVES 3)

You need:

White of 1 egg
25g (1oz) ground almonds
25g (1oz) sifted icing sugar
½ tsp almond essence
500ml (1 pint) milk
Cinnamon

To make:

1 Beat egg white until stiff.

2 Fold in almonds, essence and sugar.

3 Bring milk just to boil. Gently whisk into egg white mixture.

4 Serve in 3 cups. Sprinkle tops lightly with cinnamon.

THE SUSSEX CAROL

On Christmas night all Christians sing
To hear the news the angels bring,
On Christmas night all Christians sing,
To hear the news the angels bring—
News of great joy, news of great mirth,
News of our merciful King's birth.

Then why should men on earth be so sad,
Since our Redeemer made us glad,
Then why should men on earth be so sad,
Since our Redeemer made us glad,
When from our sins he set us free
All for to gain our liberty?

All out of darkness we have light,
Which made the angels sing this night;
All out of darkness we have light,
Which made the angels sing this night:
'Glory to God and peace to men
Now and for evermore. Amen'

TRADITIONAL ENGLISH

73

A KING IS BORN
CELEBRATE WITH A PARTY

A time to rejoice

During the seventeenth century, there were attempts to put an end to Christmas festivities in England. The ruling Puritans disapproved of what they saw as its pagan practices and 'popish' rituals. In England, an Act of Parliament banned all feasting and merrymaking on Christmas Day. Even going to church was forbidden. Puritan settlers in America tried to substitute Thanksgiving Day for Christmas; those in Massachusetts even went so far as to insist that people must work on Christmas Day itself.

Thankfully, all efforts to stamp out Christmas ended in failure. The traditions of Christmas are very dear to people, and the heart of the festival is ample cause for rejoicing and celebration.

After all, the angels announced the coming of God's only Son as good news of great joy for *all* people. There must have been a party in heaven that night.

'Let Israel rejoice
in their Maker;
let the people of Zion be glad
in their King.
Let them praise his name
with dancing
and make music to him
with tambourine and harp.
For the Lord takes delight
in his people;
He crowns the humble
with salvation.'

PSALM 149:2–4

"*Parties? They're all very well unless you happen to be the poor soul who lives next door. My neighbour had one the other night. No consideration whatsoever. Instead of keeping them indoors he has them all crowding into this barn he's got. (You can see it from our window.)*

I said it was fancy dress but naturally Rebecca (the wife) won't believe me. First this couple turn up with a donkey. Then just as we're getting to sleep there's a whole crowd in shepherd costumes (they even parked their sheep outside). Well, that was it. I went down in my slippers and banged on the door.

Next thing I know they want me to join the party. I hurried back to Rebecca, 'It's a baby boy,' I told her. 'In the barn next door. Come down and see! They say he's going to save us all. Can you believe it?'

She didn't, of course. Some people just don't like parties."

PARTIES AND ENTERTAINING

Christmas is the season of hospitality and festivity. As we remember the birth of Christ, we share the celebration with our families, friends and neighbours. Children and adults alike love a Christmas party. But the thought of all that preparation: the cooking, the invitations, the ideas for games or entertainment, can easily defeat us before we've started.

With a little advance planning, organizing a Christmas party need not be such a difficult task. In this chapter are all the ingredients you need for a party everyone will remember.

If you are planning a party, however small, it is obviously not enough just to name the day, and expect things to happen of their own accord when the guests arrive. Equally, the hosts that fuss around their party guests, constantly asking if they are enjoying themselves, will soon succeed in dampening the atmosphere. The secret is to prepare well beforehand, so that the event seems to have a life of its own when the time comes. In any case, it is wise to start making your plans and sending out invitations by the beginning of December, if you want everyone to be there.

To guarantee an event that is out of the ordinary, why not choose a theme for your party? There are three Christmas themes suggested in the following pages, or you may prefer to choose your own. Once you have your theme, choosing decorations, food and entertainment will come more easily. You could ask your guests to come dressed in costumes to suit the theme. It's surprising how many people who protest they haven't got anything suitable arrive in ingenious home-made fancy dress. And having entered into the fun, people seem to mix better when wearing something more flamboyant than their everyday clothes.

Whether your guests are in fancy dress or not, make sure they receive a warm welcome. Hang a Christmas wreath or balloons on the door, and be around to welcome each guest personally. When everyone has arrived it's good to have some sort of ice-breaker event planned, especially if people don't know each other. A game that mixes people is useful, or one where they must move around the house finding answers to questions. When you are planning games, bear in mind the people who are coming, and include some sitting-down games as well as more active ones. For a children's party, games with movement and excitement are usually a hit, but it's wise to include one or two where you can get your breath back!

A familiar complaint from party hosts is that there is so much food left over at the end. If you have spent all day cooking it's especially disheartening. To avoid this danger, go for lots of small dishes that people can pick at, rather than huge joints of meat and heavy sweets. Take some care over the presentation. A buffet that looks inviting and delicious is one that is guaranteed to get eaten. Using disposable plates, cutlery and napkins saves on breakages, and looks effective if you choose two colours that tone well. Additional touches such as lighted candles, holly or dried flowers and bowls of sweets will complete the effect.

Finally, when everyone has had their fill of cake and one or two are showing signs of tiring, it's time to fill everybody's glass and wish them all a peaceful and happy Christmas.

A party for children

Jesus was born into poverty, and his mother had to wrap him in strips of cloth rather than a silken shawl. Nevertheless he was the King of heaven. Magi from the east came to bow before him, and the Bible tells us that one day every king and prince will kneel at his feet.

Since Christmas is about celebrating Jesus' birthday, why not hold a royal banquet this year to mark the occasion? Children will love dressing up as kings and queens, princes and princesses.

Dressing up

Children need not dress up for the party, but as they arrive, present them all with a crown party hat (see page 51) and remind them that this is a royal party. Invitations can be sent out edged with a gold border and suitably worded.

Decorating the royal palace

You may not think your home looks much like a palace, but luckily children are gifted with vivid imaginations! Use gold, silver and red, traditionally royal colours. Since a children's party inevitably is messy, use disposable tableware and decorate with gold and silver sticky stars. Decorate a paper table-cloth with a design of gold crowns, using a card template. Red napkins and drinking straws, with red and silver balloons hanging from the ceiling, will add a touch of regal colour.

The banquet

Food and drink for children's parties need not be too elaborate. A bowl of crisps is often the most popular thing. Nevertheless, a little imagination will go a long way in presenting a royal banquet that will satisfy the most demanding monarch. If the children are old enough to read, label the dishes with royal-sounding titles:

★ The royal fleet—French bread 'boats' with pizza topping and cheese sails on cocktail sticks.

★ My lady's fingers—bread cut into fingers with favourite toppings.

★ Drummer boys—chicken drumsticks.

★ Crown jewels—fruit salad in wafer 'caskets'.

★ Queen's cake—fruit cake decorated with a gold paper crown around the edges, and cherry jewels.

★ King's treasure—ice cream decorated with chocolate 'gold coins'.

★ Sparkling wine—fizzy lemonade, cherryade or apple juice.

Royal games

Hunt the jewels

A treasure hunt is always popular with children. In this case, the jewels can be brightly-coloured sweets, wrapped in cellophane twists. For younger children, simply hide these around the house, taking care to choose places that are on the right eye level.

Older children may prefer a more taxing version of the game. Write a number of clues and hide them around the house so that one clue leads to the next. Clues should be fairly simple, for instance, 'Where you wipe your feet' (doormat) or 'See yourself in the bathroom' (mirror). Children may like to work in pairs to follow the clues. When they have read a clue they must replace it where they found it. The winners are the first pair to find the jewels.

Musical thrones

A stately version of musical chairs. A number of chairs are placed in the middle of the room—one less than there are children. When the music begins (something appropriate like the Brandenburg Concertos!) the children must process around the room, walking as dignified kings and queens. When the music stops, dignity is thrown to the wind and there is a mad scramble to sit on a throne. The one left without a seat is out of the game. Take away another throne each time someone is out, until you are left with a winner.

The royal ring

Thread a ring onto a long piece of string which is then knotted to form a circle. One child stands in the middle, and the other children form a circle facing her, holding the string in front of them. The child in the

middle closes her eyes for a count of ten, while the others begin passing the ring rapidly from hand to hand. When she opens her eyes she can call, 'Stop!' at any time, and she must then guess who has the ring. If she guesses right, the holder swops places with her; if not, she must try again.

Blind butler

An extremely silly and messy game, which children usually love for just that reason. Ask for two volunteers, who should be equipped with large aprons to cover their clothes. They sit opposite each other and are blindfolded. In one hand they are given spoons, and in the other a bowl of broken biscuits, cereal or rice pudding (depending on how much mess you can face).

The object of the game is quite simple—they must try to feed each other, with the help (or otherwise) of the audience.

His Majesty says

An old favourite, good to calm children down if they are getting over-excited.

One player becomes His Majesty (or Her Majesty if it is a girl). His Majesty can command his courtiers to do anything he likes, and they must obey. If the order is, 'His Majesty says, "Scratch your head" or 'His Majesty says, "Shake one leg," ' then they must obey. However, should he just say, 'Blow your nose,' then they must ignore the command and continue as they were. Only commands prefaced with 'His majesty says . . .' should be obeyed. The object is to catch players out. After a while, someone who has not been caught out takes a turn at becoming His Majesty.

SNOWY WHITE CHRISTMAS
DINNER PARTY

'I'm dreaming of a white Christmas
Just like the ones we used to know.'

IRVING BERLIN

For a dinner party that brings a touch of elegance to a festive occasion, why not choose a white Christmas theme? Only a few countries are actually guaranteed a Christmas with snow on the rooftops and window ledges, but the tradition of a white Christmas remains strong in America and Europe, even persisting on Christmas cards in sun-scorched Australia. Whether you are having a white Christmas outside or not, this party guarantees a warm evening indoors for a group of friends.

Invitations

Fancy dress is not necessary, although you may like to invite your guests to include something white in what they wear. Imaginative invitations could be in the shape of a snowman with the writing in silver.

The house

White stands out from other colours in its freshness and purity, so it is not necessary to over-use it in decoration. Snow spray can be used on windows (if you don't have the real thing). White roses or mistletoe in vases will also look effective. If you already have decorations, such as a Christmas wreath, just add white silk bows.

The focus of any dinner party is the table itself, and this is where a white theme can look particularly impressive. Allow the food itself to provide the only colour, and choose a white table-cloth with matching napkins. An unusual centrepiece could be provided by frosted fruits—grapes, plums or other fruit

dipped in egg-white and caster sugar. Finally, shining glassware and white candles will produce a softly gleaming look, doubly effective when the lights are turned low.

Food for a dinner party

As you want the white theme to set off the natural colours of the food, there's no need to worry about dreaming up 'white recipes'. In choosing your menu, however, it's worth remembering that your guests may be eating turkey or goose for the rest of Christmas, so you would be well advised to look for alternative main courses. Some imaginative suggestions are in chapter 5.

After-dinner entertainment

Guests who have just eaten a satisfying meal are unlikely to want to participate in energetic games soon afterwards. Below are some games and pastimes that make good after-dinner entertainment, without demanding too much energy of the players.

The conversation quiz

With television threatening to take over in many households, the art of conversation is in danger of being lost altogether. This quiz has no winners or losers, and no correct answers. Its aim is to start conversation and discussion, so allow everyone the chance to put their view and don't worry if some questions have to be kept till next year!

★ White Christmas comes from the film 'Holiday Inn', but what, in your opinion, are the three best films of all time?

★ You can be a famous personality for one day. Who would you like to be ?

★ If you could have any major work of art— painting, sculpture or any beautiful object—in your home, which would you choose? (You may also want to discuss where you would actually put it!)

★ If you could be born into any period of history (including the present), which would you choose?

★ Supposing you can have houses in three different parts of the world, where would they be?

★ Who would you nominate as the person to have had the greatest influence on history?

★ You are hurrying to an appointment, having just taken some cash out of the bank. An elderly tramp who is weaving along the road suddenly falls over. Be honest, what would you do?

★ What is the most stupid or embarrassing thing you have ever done?

★ What, in your opinion, is the worst song ever written?

★ If you had to live on a desert island what one item would you take with you, besides the basic necessities?

I'm dreaming

A fascinating and revealing game, which will only work if some players are new to the game. Send two or three people out of the room, explaining that the rest of you are going to agree upon the story of a dream. They must discover the story when they return by asking questions. In fact you explain to those who remain that all they must do is answer the questions in the repeating sequence 'yes', 'yes', 'no'.

Call the first player in, and tell them they can only ask questions which the group can answer with yes or no. The person might begin with a question such as, 'Was I involved in this dream?', to which everyone replies with amazement 'yes!' They will then proceed to invent their own dream, without realizing what is happening. Stop the game when the dreamer is running out of questions, or begins to smell a rat. The next player can then be called in, and the same game played—with different results. Note: victims for this game should be chosen for their vivid imaginations and strong sense of humour!

White chocolate race

A fun game in which adults can become as greedy as children. Be sure to avoid playing it straight after dinner, though, or enthusiasm may be lacking.

You need a bar of white chocolate, a dice, knife and fork and some clothes—a silly hat, scarf and outsize gloves such as motorcycling gloves. Players sit round in a circle, and throw the dice in turn. When someone throws a six, they are allowed to eat some chocolate. The catch is that they must first put on the hat, scarf and gloves, and then eat using the knife and fork. Meanwhile the other players keep throwing the dice and can interrupt the first player if they throw a six. Even non-chocolate addicts have been known to get excited in this game.

ONE·WORLD PARTY

At Christmas we celebrate the birth of the Prince of Peace, so what better time to give a party which celebrates the world-wide family of nations? A party with an international flavour offers an unusual alternative at Christmas and also provides an excuse to sample recipes and games from all over the world. The ideas for this party are suitable for adults and children.

Costume

You may like to invite everyone to come in the national dress of a different country. Most costumes aren't too difficult to find or make: a cowboy outfit for America, a classical robe (made from a sheet) for Greece, a kilt for

Decorations

In addition to the usual Christmas decorations, why not hang the colourful flags of different countries around the room? You may be able to buy small flags, or get children to help make them with paper and poster paints. Small flags could also provide decoration for a cold buffet or, if you're planning a sit-down meal, place settings. If you have souvenirs from abroad, such as fans from Japan or Spain, they could add to the international atmosphere.

International cuisine

A 'one-world' party offers endless scope to cooks. In fact, the problem is likely to be

Scotland, or a sari for India. If you'd prefer a simpler alternative, you could ask guests to come wearing hats that suggest different countries—berets, baseball caps, bowlers, turbans or Russian fur hats. A prize could be awarded at the end of the evening for the best-dressed guest.

knowing which dishes to leave out. Again, it's best to place the accent on a wide variety of light dishes so that people can sample different tastes from around the world. You could even ask guests to bring a dish from the country they represent. It will make for an interesting buffet supper and save you doing all the cooking!

Some food and drink ideas for a buffet are:
Pizza, pasta salad, Russian salad, spring rolls, beef or vegetable samosas, pate and French sticks, German sausage, cheeses from around the world, chocolate brownies, Apfelstrudel, Danish pastries, pumpkin pie, blueberry pie, Neapolitan ice cream, Turkish delight, Turkish coffee, Jamaican punch, Indian or China tea.

Games without frontiers

Musical hats

This would make a good starter game, especially if you have asked people to come wearing hats from different countries. If not,

hat off the person in front and put it on their own head. The hats keep moving around the circle until the music stops. Whoever is without a hat on their head at this point is out of the game. Take away another hat each time you restart, until finally you're left with two players swopping one hat. The player wearing the hat when the music stops is the winner.

Antony and Cleopatra

Another ideal game for getting people to mix and meet each other. Think of as many famous pairs from different countries as you can—Antony and Cleopatra, Gilbert and Sullivan, Napoleon and Josephine, Mickey and Minnie Mouse, Laurel and Hardy and so on.

Make separate name tags for each

you'll need a bag of hats of any kind, enough for everyone at the party. Distribute the hats amongst the players and ask them to stand in a circle wearing their hats. Have some music ready to play, but before you begin, take a hat off one player so that you are one short. When the music starts, each player must take the

character, and stick or pin one on the back of each player. (Make sure you have an even number playing the game.) The idea is for each player to find the other half of their pair. They must first discover who their character is by moving around the room asking questions of other players. Questions can only be given a yes or no answer—such as 'Am I still alive?' When two players think they belong together, they can go to a third and ask, 'Are we a pair?' If they are right they can drop out and watch. The game ends when everyone has found their right partner.

Chinese whispers

A traditional game, that can be played with everyone sitting in a line or a circle. The more players, the more fun and confusion will result. One player begins the game by whispering a message to the person next to them. The message should be only a sentence long but as difficult as possible to understand and repeat—for example 'Does this shop stock short socks with spots?' The next person must pass on the message exactly as they heard it to their neighbour. Players must whisper in their neighbour's ear and are not allowed to ask for the message to be repeated. When the message reaches the last player they must repeat out loud what they received. Probably something like, 'Does this ship shock sore soggy sharks?'

All together now . . .

Divide everyone into groups of four or five people. Explain that the object of the game is to think of as many songs as possible which mention place names, for example: 'Tulips from Amsterdam', 'London Bridge is falling down' or 'We're bound for Botany Bay'.

Each team sings as a group, singing only the line from their song which mentions the name of a place. Team 1 begins, and as soon as they finish, Team 2 must come in with a different song, followed by Team 3 and so on, back to Team 1 again. If a team cannot think of a song immediately—or if they repeat one that has already been used—they are out. The winning team is the last one left in.

What country am I?

This game is really a fast form of charades, calling for quick thinking on the part of the players. An umpire with a list of well-known countries divides people into teams, and asks each team to send one person to get the name of a country. They must then go and act it to their team without using words. For example if the country is Australia they might try and convey kangaroos, boomerangs or surfing. As soon as someone guesses the country correctly, the team can send another player to get the next name on the list. The winning team is the one to get to the end of the list first.

GOOD CHRISTIANS ALL, REJOICE!

Good Christians all, rejoice
With heart and soul and voice;
Give ye heed to what we say;
News! News!
Jesus Christ is born today!
Ox and ass before Him bow,
He is in the manger now;
Christ is born today!
Christ is born today!

Good Christians all, rejoice
With heart and soul and voice;
Now ye hear of endless bliss:
Joy! Joy!
Jesus Christ was born for this!
He hath oped the heavenly door,
And man is blessed for evermore;
Christ was born for this!
Christ was born for this!

GERMAN—14TH CENTURY
TRANSLATED BY JOHN MASON NEALE (1818–66)

THE BIG EVENT

O COME, LET US ADORE HIM

'So Joseph also went up from the town of Nazareth in Galilee to Judea, to Bethlehem, the town of David, because he belonged to the house and line of David. He went there to register with Mary, who was pledged to be married to him and was expecting a child. While they were there, the time came for the baby to be born, and she gave birth to her firstborn, a son. She wrapped him in strips of cloth and placed him in a manger because there was no room for them in the inn.'

LUKE 2:4–7

Joseph and Mary are seen little in the Gospels after their centre-stage part in the birth stories. It is certain that no event in the rest of their lives could have compared with the memory of how Jesus came into the world, announced by angels and worshipped by strangers.

Today, adults and children all over the world relive the memory of that birth every year, by holding their own Christmas events. In homes, churches, schools and hospitals, carol services and nativity plays are held to tell again the wonder of that night. In this chapter we include an original nativity play, Bible readings to outline the Christmas story, and carols, old and new, to include in your own special Christmas event.

"Every Christmas I get a few more grey hairs during rehearsals. But come the night of the nativity play, I always say it was worth it. Just to see the angels shuffle on in their flowing sheets and tinsel haloes. The kings kneeling to offer their mums' old jewellery boxes. The shepherds in their assorted striped towels making a dramatic entrance by tripping over the lead of their pull-along sheep. Joseph blushing scarlet as he puts an arm round Mary's shoulders. And Mary in the centre of it all, rocking the cardboard manger.

The girl we chose for Mary this year was as nervous as a kitten. She's one of the shy ones who tend to go unnoticed most of the time. In rehearsals, she whispered her lines as if they were a secret. But when it came to the performance night, I was glad we had given her the part. When she came on, holding the baby, her face was glowing with pride; I honestly think it was the biggest day of her life. Perhaps she knew how Mary felt."

The humble nativity play has a long and honourable history. Its earliest roots are in the re-enactments of the manger scene performed by clergy in the early Middle Ages. St Francis of Assisi and his followers took part in the first well-documented nativity play on Christmas Eve in 1223.

Today, children all over the world look forward to playing a part as an angel, a shepherd or a wise man in the nativity play. In villages in Belgium, people of all ages and even animals join in recreating the manger scene. In Hungary, the play is taken from house to house by children dressed in Biblical costume. Many nativity plays take place in schools, churches and children's clubs over Christmas time. For the proud parents, it's a special moment to watch their children step forward at the right time and present their gifts at the manger.

If you are helping to organize a nativity play for Christmas, however, there can be a lot of work involved. Where do you find a suitable script and music? How do you make the costumes? How do you run the rehearsals?

With all these problems in mind, we've included an original nativity play here, complete with script and songs. It's fun to do, and caters for a large number of children, so that there is a part for everyone to play. It can also be adapted for smaller groups, by children playing more than one part in the four different scenes. If you simply want something to keep your family amused at home, Scene I can be performed on its own by a few actors.

Plays without tears

For those attempting the full production, the key to producing a successful nativity play is to keep all the elements fairly simple. If you go for elaborate costumes and a stunning set, you may find you run out of time for rehearsing the children in their parts. Concentrate on the play itself, and if possible, recruit someone else to worry about set and costumes. Biblical dress can easily be fashioned out of stripy material cut in a basic 'T' shape with a hole for the head. The best backdrop is one that can be adapted for all purposes. A starry night sky over town rooftops would suit this play.

Divide rehearsals into the four different scenes. If possible you should have different children (apart from the narrator) involved in scenes one to three. This way you can rehearse each separately without keeping children waiting around. The songs are based on traditional carol melodies; hand the practice of them over to your musician and add them into the play at a later stage. One last word of warning—allow plenty of time. Frantic rehearsals cause frayed nerves!

A STAR OVER BETHLEHEM
A nativity play for children

Characters in order of appearance

Narrator - the Star

Three Shepherds

Sheep and Lambs

(two or three—at least one small lamb)

Angels (a choir)

Mary

Joseph

Donkey

Innkeeper

Hotelier

Citizens of Bethlehem

Stable Boy

1st Adviser to Herod

Herod

2nd Adviser to Herod

Servants and advisers in Herod's court

Three Wise Men

Scene I

(The narrator enters, dressed as a star. She might wear a silver costume, and a circlet on her head with a star attached to the front)

Narrator: Hello! I'm the star of this play. Actually I'm only a little star in the night sky. I've always wanted to be one of the big stars, in Orion, or the Plough, or the Great Bear. Then everyone would know me. But I'm only a little star, so they sent me to hang over a place called Bethlehem. It's a sleepy little town in a small country. I couldn't see why it needed its own star. The only people who seemed to be awake were some shepherds, looking after their sheep on the hillside.

(The three shepherds take the stage. They can be accompanied by one or two children on all fours, costumed as sheep.)

Shepherds *(in chorus):*
We shepherds brave who guard the sheep,
We never slumber, never sleep.
We stay out on the hills at night,
The stars above our only light.
We watch for wolves, we watch for bears,
We watch for lions from their lairs.
If something roars out in the night,
We huddle close and shake with fright.
We shepherds brave who guard the sheep,
We never slumber, never sleep.

Sheep: Baa! Baa!

Shepherd 1: Listen! What was that?

Sheep: Baa!

Shepherd 2: It was the sheep, stupid.

(Shepherd 3 yawns loudly)

Shepherd 1: Listen, that sounds like a lion.

Shepherd 3: It was me yawning, dopey.

(Shepherd 2 comes up behind Shepherd 1 and growls like a lion)

Shepherd 1 *(holding his stomach):* Ooh pardon me, everyone!

Shepherd 3: Honestly, for brave shepherds you lot are easily scared.

Shepherd 1: Who's easily scared?

Shepherd 3: You are!

Shepherd 1: You can't scare me!

Shepherd 2: No, you can't scare me either!

(They square up to each other.)

Shepherds: Oh yeah? Oh yeah? Oh yeah?

Sheep (loudly): Baa!

(The shepherds jump in the air and huddle together closely.)

Shepherds: What was that?

Shepherd 2: Oh let's get some sleep. Nothing's going to bother us tonight. Nothing ever happens round here.

(They sit down, resting against each other, and begin to snore. The sheep baa and go to lie down by the shepherds.)

Narrator: Nothing ever happens round here. That's exactly what I thought. Until I realized that the sky around me was getting brighter, and beginning to glow and hum with sound . . .

(During this the angels have entered, opposite the sleeping shepherds. Music introduces the Angels' Song. The shepherds wake up and look scared and amazed as the angels sing. The angels gradually surround them, and dance round them.)

The Angels' Song

(To the tune of 'Torches, Torches'—page 92. Start softly and grow louder)

Whisper, whisper,
Have you heard the story?
Have you heard the news
that a king is born?
Jesus, Jesus come from
glory,
Come as a babe to save
us all.

Shepherds, shepherds,
Have you heard the story?
Have you heard the news
that a king is born?
Jesus, Jesus come from
glory,
Come as a babe to save
us all.

Sing it, sing it,
Have you heard the story?
Have you heard the news that
a king is born?
Jesus, Jesus come from glory,
Come as a babe to save us all.

Shout it, shout it,
Have you heard the story?
Have you heard the news that a king is born?
Jesus, Jesus come from glory,
Come as a babe to save us all.

(Angels exit, humming the tune)

Shepherd 1: Did you hear it too?

Shepherd 2: A king is born.

Shepherd 3: His name is Jesus.

Shepherd 1: He's come to save us all.

Shepherd 2: Well, what are we waiting for? Let's go and see for ourselves!

(Shepherds exit)

Narrator: While I listened to those angels, I could feel myself grow and begin to shine brighter. Something was going to happen in Bethlehem that night. I looked down on the town to see if I could see any sign of a baby. But all I could see were two people and a donkey, plodding wearily through the streets.

Scene II

(Joseph and Mary enter, with another child, costumed as the donkey. They walk wearily to centre stage.)

Mary: Oh Joseph, I can't go any further tonight.

Joseph: Just until we've found somewhere to stay, Mary. Here, why don't you sit on the donkey?

(She does so but the donkey buckles under her weight and they both end up on the floor. Joseph helps her up)

Joseph: Oh dear—I think even our donkey is too tired to go any further. I'll knock at this door and see if they have anywhere to stay.

(He knocks and an innkeeper comes to the door.)

Innkeeper: Yes? What do you want?

Joseph: Please, sir, we need somewhere to stay for the night. We're worn out from travelling, and my wife is expecting a baby.

Innkeeper: Oh don't bother me, all my rooms are full and I'm just in the middle of cooking supper! *(He slams the door.)*

Joseph: Never mind, Mary. I expect this one will help us. *(He knocks at another door.)*

Hotelier: Good evening, sir. Bethlehem Hotel at your service.

Joseph: Er, good evening. We need somewhere to stay for the night. We're worn out from travelling, and my wife is expecting a baby.

Hotelier: I'm sorry, sir all our rooms are taken. And anyway I doubt if you could afford our prices. Have a pleasant evening, sir. *(He slams the door.)*

Mary: What are we going to do? The baby's going to come soon.

Joseph: There must be somewhere.

(They begin to trail around the stage as if trying different doors. As they do so, the citizens of Bethlehem appear, and turn them away, singing 'No Room'.)

No Room
(to the tune of 'O Christmas Tree'—page 92)

Walk by our street, walk by our street,
No room for you, no food to eat.
Walk by our street, walk by our street,
No room for you, no food to eat.
But we are full, we're warm in bed;
We're glad it's you, not us instead.
Walk by our street, walk by our street,
No room for you, no food to eat.

O see the signs, O see the signs;
All rooms are taken, especially mine.
O see the signs, O see the signs;
All rooms are taken, especially mine.
Don't knock the door, I'm trying to sleep
And what I have, I'd like to keep.
O see the signs, O see the signs;
All rooms are taken, especially mine.

(The citizens exit.)

Mary: Oh Joseph, we've tried everywhere.

I can't go any further.

(She lies down.)

Joseph: Mary! We can't stop here. What about the baby?

(Enter a stable boy.)

Stable Boy: Please sir, do you need somewhere to stay?

Joseph: Please. Anywhere!

Stable Boy: I only look after my master's animals but he lets me sleep in the stable with them. It's not very clean, but it's warm.

Joseph: You're very kind. Please show us the way.

(They help Mary up and exit together.)

Stable Boy: I'm sorry it's all I've got to give you.

(Music can play refrain of 'No Room' as they exit.)

Narrator: Poor lost things. Only a stable to sleep in. But the angels had sung about a baby being born in Bethlehem that night. Surely they couldn't mean one born in a stable? I looked down and saw the city of Jerusalem, and a gleaming palace sitting on a hill. Perhaps the baby come to save us all would be born there.

Scene III

(Herod's palace. Herod sits on a throne surrounded by servants and advisers. Two slaves cool him with large feather fans on poles.)

1st Adviser: His Majesty King Herod!

(A fanfare. Herod stands up.)

Herod: My name is Herod, but you can call me . . . Herod the Great.

All *(bowing down):* Oh Great and Glorious Majesty!

Herod: Or Herod the Wise.

All: Oh Wise and Wonderful Majesty!

Herod: Or I don't mind Herod the Handsome.

All: Oh Handsome and He-man Majesty!

2nd Adviser: What about Herod the Merciful?

Herod: Guards! Off with his head!

2nd Adviser: No, no, just a joke, your Majesty!

1st Adviser: If your Majesty pleases, there are some wise men to see you.

Herod: Wise men? Off with their heads!

2nd Adviser: But your Majesty, it's something about a new king.

Herod: What? I'm the only king round here. Show them in.

(1st Adviser goes, and returns with the wise men.)

Herod: Where do you come from and what do you want?

Wise Men *(in chorus):*
Your Majesty, we've travelled far,
We come from the East and follow a star,
We search for a king, but we know it's not you,
This king is a baby, all tiny and new.
We've bought him three presents to lay
at his feet,
So we need his address, or the name
of the street.

Herod: How interesting! Let me just ask my advisers if they know. *(In an undertone)* I'll have the guards chop off their heads and feed them to the royal ducks.

Adviser 1 *(in an undertone):* No, no, your Majesty. We need to know where this baby is.

Adviser 2 *(in an undertone):* Use them to lead us to the baby.

Herod *(in an undertone):* Good idea.
(Addressing the wise men):
Oh wise men, when you do find this baby king let me know. I've got a present for him too.

Wise Men: Yes, your Majesty.

(The wise men bow and exit)

Herod: My present will be his death. Ha ha ha! I'm Herod the Cruel.

All *(bowing):* Oh Cunning and Cruel Majesty!

(Herod and his court exit)

Narrator: Well, the angels did talk about a king, but I didn't think that could be him. Herod the Headcase, I would have called him. The only baby I'd heard of was coming into the world in a dirty stable that night. So that was where I returned. And do you know, I had a funny feeling those wise men were following me. They kept pointing in my direction. Nobody's ever bothered to point at me before!

Scene IV

(The stable scene with Mary, Joseph and the child in a manger. Music such as 'Away in a Manger' can play as the scene changes. Joseph and Mary sit by the manger. The stable boy enters and indicates that someone is coming. The shepherds enter. They bow to Joseph and Mary and kneel beside the manger with their sheep.)

Shepherds:
Us poor shepherds, we hope you'll excuse,
A choir of angels told us the news.
O child from heaven, we've brought a gift, too,
A little lamb, new-born like you.

Lamb: Baa!

(Mary thanks them and strokes the lamb. The shepherds stand to one side of the manger. Next the stable boy introduces the wise men with their gifts. They bow to everyone, and also kneel beside the manger.)

Wise Men:
O infant king, we've travelled far,
We come from the East and follow a star.

We bring three gifts to lay at your feet,
Frankincense, gold and myrrh, bitter-sweet.

(The wise men take their places around the manger, and Mary and Joseph stand up.)

Joseph: For each of your gifts we thank you all.

Mary: Now see my son Jesus, all wrapped in a shawl.

(Mary lifts the baby out of the manger to show them.)

Narrator: And they all gathered round—the shepherds, the wise men and the stable boy. I was the only one who couldn't see him. As usual everyone had forgotten me. So I moved in the sky until I was right overhead and I looked in through a hole in the stable roof.

(She comes round behind the manger and everyone parts so that the audience can see her.)

Then I could see him, the Saviour child, and I felt myself grow, and beam brighter than I had ever done before.

Wise Man: Look, it's the star! The star that we followed to find the way here. It too wants to worship the infant king.

Mary: What a beautiful star!

(The rest of the cast join them for the final song.)

What a Gift
(to the tune of 'Silent Night'—page 92)

Christmas night, stars so bright
Look upon wondrous sight.
> *Star shines over stable small,*
> *A child is born to save us all.*
> *Born to save us all!*
> *Born to save us all!*

> *Christmas night, stars so bright*
> *Look upon wondrous sight.*
> *Angels sing of peace on earth,*
> *Worshipping the Saviour's birth.*
> *Saviour born for me!*
> *Saviour born for me!*

Christmas night, stars so bright
Look upon wondrous sight.
What a gift is sent from heaven,
Jesus, God's own son, is given.
Light has dawned upon earth!
Light has dawned upon earth!

Narrator: And that was the night I was sent to shine over a stable, in a sleepy little town called Bethlehem. The night God's own son was given. Now I don't mind that I'm not a big star, or part of Orion or the Plough or the Bear. The other stars know me as the Star of Bethlehem.

The Angel's Song

Tune: Torches, Torches

Whis-per, whis-per, have you heard the sto-ry? Have you heard the news that a King is born?

Je - sus, Je - sus, Co - me fr - om glo-ry, Co - me as a babe to - save us all

No Room

Tune: O Christmas Tree (Germany)

Walk by our street. Walk by our street. No room for you, no food to eat. Walk

by our street. Walk by our street. No food for you, no food to eat. But we are full, we're

warm in bed. We're glad it's you, not us ins-tead. Walk by our street, Walk by our street. No

room for you. No food to eat.

What a Gift

Tune: Silent Night (Germany)

Capo 1

Chri - st - mas night, sta - rs so bright. Look up - on won - drous sight

Star shines o - ver sta - ble small. A child is bo - rn to sa - ve us all.

Born to sa - ve us a - ll. Bo - rn to sa - ve us all.

THE WHOLE STORY
Nine Lessons and Carols

This selection of nine Bible readings, or lessons, follows the story of God's dealings with people; from the Garden of Eden, through the foretelling of the birth of Jesus in the Old Testament, and the Gospel descriptions of how it happened in the New Testament, to John's famous passage about Jesus which starts 'In the beginning was the Word...' These lessons are traditionally used to form the shape of a Christmas Eve service of nine lessons and carols.

The most famous of these services is broadcast each year across the world from King's College Chapel, Cambridge, by the BBC.

You could use the outline below for any formal Christmas celebration at your workplace, school or church. The suggested carols can be found in almost any collection of traditional carols. You can, however, choose whatever you feel best fits your particular occasion.

1 *Genesis 3:1–15*
In the Garden of Eden
'O Come All Ye Faithful'

2 *Genesis 22:15–18*
God's promise to bless Abraham's family
'O come, O come Emmanuel'

3 *Isaiah 9:2, 6–7*
Christ's birth and kingdom foretold

4 *Isaiah 11:1–9*
Justice and peace in Christ's reign foretold
'Once in Royal David's City'

5 *Luke 1: 26–38*
The angel Gabriel visits Mary

6 *Luke 2:1–7*
The birth of Jesus
'Away in a Manger'

7 *Luke 2:8–16*
The shepherds go to the manger
'While Shepherds Watched'

8 *Matthew 2: 1–11*
The wise men visit Jesus
'We Three Kings'

9 *John 1:1–14*
The mystery of God becoming a human being